Towson

By H. George Hahn and Carl Behm III

Foreword by P. W. Filby
Donning Co./Publishers
Norfolk, Virginia

The jail trestle of the Ma & Pa, 1941.
Photograph courtesy of Charles T. Mahan

A PICTORIAL HISTORY OF A MARYLAND TOWN

Towson

Library of Congress Cataloging in Publication Data:

Hahn, Henry George, 1942-
Towson: a pictorial history of a Maryland town.
1. Towson, Md.—History. I. Behm, Carl, 1942-
joint author.
F189.T6H33   975.2'71   77-20052
ISBN 0-915442-36-1

Printed in the United States of America

Contents

Photograph by Carl Behm III

York Road, 1894.

*Photograph courtesy of
Sheppard-Pratt Hospital*

For Cynthia
and
For Susan, Jennifer, and Justin

Foreword

Since many areas in Maryland have been treated historically, it is surprising that Towson has never been the object of a study. Fortunately, when its history finally came to be written, the task fell to H. George Hahn and Carl Behm. Both men are professors of Towson State University, an institution that has itself been an important part of Towson's development.

Towson: A Pictorial History of a Maryland Town traces the archetypal evolution of an American community from its rural beginnings to its urban present. In doing so, it provides an excellent introduction for layman and scholar alike. Of course, the historical text alone would make this a good book for almost every home in Towson. But the heart of the book is its more than 300 high quality photographs. A kaleidoscope of pictures, captions, and historical commentary, this history will be welcomed not only in Towson but also in Baltimore and elsewhere in Maryland.

P. W. Filby, Director
Maryland Historical Society
Baltimore, Maryland
September 28, 1976

Sheppard-Pratt at the turn of the century.
*Photograph courtesy of
Sheppard-Pratt Hospital*

Preface

Any history is ultimately a scrapbook of
documents and memories. It is only the quality
of continuity among them that makes the
history good or bad. This is especially true of
pictorial histories, for the writer is bound to the
graphics which have become available to him.
But therein lies the value of the pictorial history
as well. The pictures force the historian to
work from the bottom up, to be ever the faithful
observer of the records that have come down to
him from the past. Only after he establishes a base
in photographic fact do themes and an
arrangement emerge.

The themes are various: roads, families,
architectural styles, dress, transportation, and
institutions. Arranging them into a whole is
comparable to showing a scrapbook to a friend.
Each picture suggests a story to be told.

As a result, this book is composed of many
sections, as a quilt is made of many patches.
The story of the Ma & Pa Railroad, for example,
begins in 1882 when the line reached Towson. It
is told without interruption until the last train
leaves in 1958. Only then does the section on
the Church of the Immaculate Conception,
founded in 1884, begin. This double chronology
runs throughout the book. The underlying
movement is forward, the slow progression of
Towson's history. Within it, there is the
"speeded up" chronology of an individual
section.

Photograph by Carl Behm III

I. "Barons And Burghers"

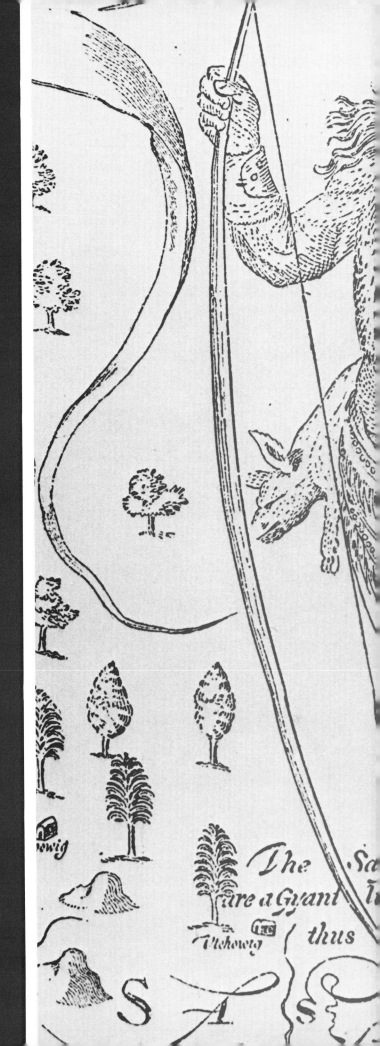

"They seemed like giants to the English":
Thus Captain John Smith described the
Susquehannoughs during his 1608 exploratory
voyage up the Chesapeake Bay. Some wore
"cassocks made of beares' head and skinnes"
and "one had the head of a wolfe hanging in a
chaine for a jewell." Smith's account stresses
the size and the fearsomeness of the largest of
the gigantic Indians, "the calf of whose leg was
three-quarters of a yard about, and all the rest
of his limbes so answerable to that proportion,
that he seemed the goodliest man we ever
beheld. His hayre the one side was long, the
other shave close, with a ridge over his crowne
like a cock's combe. His arrows were five
quarters long, headed with the splinters of a
white, chrystall-like stone, in form of a heart, an
inch broad, and an inch and a halfe or more
long. These he wore in a wolve's skinne at his
backe for his quiver, his bow in the one hand
and his club in the other, as is described."

*From Scharf's **History of Maryland***

es= ahanougs
peop le &
red

G V E

The Susquehannoughs: A People of War

The land that eventually became Towson was first the hunting grounds of the Susquehannough Indians, a fierce band of warriors whose chief settlement was near the mouth of the Susquehanna River, but whose domain included a large part of the eastern and western shores of the Chesapeake, including all of Baltimore County.

From the beginning of settlement in southern Maryland, the Susquehannoughs did not accept the arrival of the white man with the passivity of the less warlike tribes of southern Maryland. Consequently, on September 13, 1642, the Governor of the Colony declared the Susquehannoughs "enemies to the province and as such to be reputed and proceeded against by all persons." Although the Susquehannoughs officially sued for peace ten years later, early settlers in Baltimore County were not safe from attack. For war was in the blood of the Susquehannoughs, whose name has been conjectured to mean "people of bounty obtained in war." Their culture was based on the hunt and the raid. Prior to an expedition, the warriors would decorate their bodies with paint and feathers, and as chants extolled the bravery of the tribe they would mime the tomahawking and scalping of their enemies. It was not to be expected that settlers whose cabins lay in close proximity to the trails by which the Susquehannoughs moved south to harvest oysters from the saltwater or to seize women from the Piscataways would be passed unmolested. Settlers were killed, their cabins plundered and burned, their gardens uprooted, their weapons stolen.

Yet the settlers prevailed. Smallpox, brought to America with the colonists, decimated the Susquehannoughs. By 1673 the proud tribe, which by John Smith's account of 1608 had been able to assemble as many as six hundred warriors, could barely muster three hundred men. Repeated attacks by their traditional enemy, the Iroquois, further weakened the Susquehannoughs, who attempted to defend themselves in their palisaded villages. Finally, the Iroquois overcame the last resistance of the tribe, and the Relation of Maryland of 1676-1677 describes the Susquehannoughs as utterly exterminated.

By the end of the seventeenth century the land north of Baltimore was comparatively safe for settlement, and as the new century began, the original land grants in the Towson area were being surveyed. The age of the roaming hunter and warrior passed. The age of farming and construction began.

Wild Country and Early Land Grants

The most important of Towson's eighteenth-century settlers were the Towson brothers, Thomas and William, who in 1752 made camp on a ridge seven miles north of the small town of Baltimore. As dawn rose on their campsite, they saw around them a wooded countryside interspersed with streams, valleys, and meadows, all bisected by a winding Indian trail, now Joppa Road. These German brothers— some say English—had come to Pennsylvania, but finding it unsuitable, pushed south into Maryland. Perhaps the increasing prejudice against the Germans by the English settlers had caused the move, or perhaps it was just restless spirit. Regardless, industry and a sense of opportunity characterized their remaining on this hill in Maryland. They cut down trees, cleared the land, and built a log house near the spot where the Towson Theater now stands.

The land the Towson brothers surveyed was wild but not unclaimed. If we imagine the present York Road as a stem, we can see that on it once clustered a number of land grants, larger at top and bottom, and of middling size at the

center, or at what is now Towson proper.

To the south was Job Evans' "Friends' Discovery," granted to him in 1654 by the King's Law Office. In 1755 William Govane bought the eastern five hundred acres and called them "Drumquhasel."

To the north was "Northampton," a 1,500-acre tract acquired in 1695 by Colonel Henry Darnall, a member of Lord Baltimore's Council. It was Darnall's family that sold the entire parcel to Charles Ridgely, Merchant, in 1745.

At the center, five land grants divided the area that would become Towson proper. The common point of these tracts was "at a bounded white oak standing in the head of a great glade on the south of Setter Hill." This marked tree stood at what is now the northeast corner of Delaware and Shealey Avenues.

The first and largest of these central tracts was "James's Meadows," a two hundred-acre parcel surveyed in 1703 for Thady O. Tracy. It was from this tract in 1752 that the Towson family bought five to eight acres. They farmed the land and later built an inn.

Two years later Tracy had surveyed a second tract, "Tracy's Parke." In 1706 Thomas

McNamara acquired a third tract of 150 acres, which he called "Gunner's Range," possibly because of good hunting in the area. It may have been there that Thomas Towson earned his reputation as a crack marksman. McNamara, however, was apparently not interested in hunting on the land, for he sold out promptly to the surveyor James Crook.

After a lapse of thirty-nine years in local grants, William Pearce patented in 1745 "Molly's Industry," where today Hutzler's store stands. The Towsons also purchased acreage in this tract.

The last of Towsontown's early land grants, "Gott's Hope" was laid out for Richard Gott in 1753. Ten years later the portion of this tract adjacent to "Molly's Industry" was sold to William Pearce, who aptly dubbed the sliver "Pearce's Security." That wedge is the site of the Valley Gun Shop.

In the next one hundred years, the press of people from Baltimore and Pennsylvania turned the old land grants into new farms, roads, and businesses, including an inn.

An Inn at the Crossroads

When the Towson brothers selected their homestead, they showed the foresight of born entrepreneurs. The Joppa Road was the principal artery connecting central Baltimore County with the port and county seat at Joppa. In addition, a road linking the rich farmland of southern Pennsylvania with the port of Baltimore had been completed in 1743, less than ten years before the brothers' arrival. In the first month of its existence this road carried "no less than sixty wagons" of flaxseed to Baltimore, a sign of the future importance of the York Road.

Perhaps from the beginning the Towsons conceived of establishing a business which would take advantage of this traffic. Perhaps some trade was done. We cannot know for sure, but we do know that in 1768 Ezekiel Towson, William's son, built a stone tavern near where Hutzler's is now. A document of the court of 1768 shows the inn well prepared to serve travelers. Its bill of fare of two dozen items included the following, priced in pounds, shillings, and pence:

Stableage with good Clover or
  Timothy Hay per Night & Day
  or 24 Hours 0.2.0
Wine & Beer from London or Bristol 0.1.6
a Hot Meale of Roast or broiled
  with Small Beer Cyder 0.1.6
Breakfast or Supper 0.1.0
Toddy made of Country Rum or
  Brandy per Quart 0.0.8
Lodging per night with clean Sheets 0.0.6

The success of the tavern hung in the balance in 1799 when the road to York was being fashioned into a turnpike. The original plans called for the turnpike to pass "thirty-two perches" from the tavern. Petitioning the Maryland legislature to change the route, Ezekiel Towson noted that he had kept his tavern many years "for the entertainment of man and beast." If the lawmakers would route the road past his door, he promised to donate any land needed for such a change. Alone, the innkeeper inaugurated the venerable Towsonian tradition of private gain by political transaction. The direction of the York Turnpike was changed, and Towsontown and its tavern thrived. Ezekiel prepared his inn for an increased patronage.

The Towson Tavern soon boasted thirteen bedrooms on the second and third floors as well as a first-floor dining room, bar, kitchen, pantry, reading room, lobby, and private quarters for Ezekiel and his twelve children. (Ezekiel apparently was never at a loss for household help.) It is said that among the boarders at various times were Washington (of course) Lafayette, and members of the touring Prussian royal house, who were stranded in the Towson Tavern for many days during a snowstorm.

When the Towson family scattered and Ezekiel died, the inn was sold and resold to many proprietors during the next century. Edward H. Ady, whose tenure dominated the

The inn in the 1920s.

Photograph courtesy of Jennie E. Jessop

The oldest house in central Towson, Solomon Schmuck's dwelling was built about 1787. A Baltimorean, Schmuck had married into the Towson family. The home was later occupied by Samuel Kirk, the silversmith.

Photograph by Carl Behm III

second half of the 1800s, was an especially popular hosteler. He supplied fresh vegetables from his own garden, milk and cheese from his dairy, meat from his farm, and wine and grapes from his arbor.

Business increased when two lines of omnibuses started "immediately from the door." And when Towson was selected as county seat in 1854, a "plank road" was built from the tavern to the new Court House. At Ady's tavern jurymen boarded, attorneys lunched, and politicians blustered.

As the nation moved toward civil war, Southern sympathizers and Union men gathered at Ady's. As a result, debates on national issues were inevitable. The Ridgelys declaimed for States' Rights and the Chews for the Union cause. One heated debate in 1861 ended with the grinding of sabres on the whetstone behind the tavern. Harry Gilmor sharpened his for the South and Sam Whittle his for the North.

The Tavern witnessed the war in other ways, too. On June 11, 1861, a detachment of Federal troopers stationed at Cockeysville demanded from Ady all the arms in his possession. He handed them five sabres on loan from the state to the Baltimore County Horse Guards. After a thorough search the soldiers found no other weapons. In 1864 Harry Gilmor, by then a major in the Confederate Cavalry, lifted a glass in his old home tavern during his foray across Baltimore County. Because he did

not charge Gilmor for his ale, Ady was arrested on the charge of giving aid to the enemy.

Through the nineteenth century and into the twentieth, farmers with produce and livestock moving south along the York Turnpike to Baltimore City would stop at the Towson Tavern before setting out on the last leg of their journey. For those driving a herd, the grazing field that Ady provided was apt recompense for sleeping four to a bed, sixteen to a room.

Nor was social life neglected during the Ady years. The proprietor gave dances once a month for the town. The swinging doors of the two front rooms were kept open to lend a ballroom flavor as gallants and belles danced and sang.

Activity continued until the Towson Tavern was razed in 1929. After a life of 161 years, not only a tavern but a mute hall of records was demolished.

In construction from 1783 to 1790, Hampton House is a classic example of the late Georgian style. Built with stone quarried from the estate and bricks imported from England, Hampton is a blend of the ethics of old world landed aristocracy and of new world business.

The main block and its two-story wings echo the old world symmetry and stability that underline the theme of order in the country, the garden fashioned from the wild. Its cupola lends vantage, light and power to the structure. From it the Ridgelys may have watched their ships sail into the Baltimore harbor. The very structure of Hampton suggests a pattern of eighteenth-century American history: wealth of land crowned by further wealth in trade.

Photograph by Jack Avery

Charles Ridgely (1733-1790). The builder of Hampton House served as a member of the Maryland House of Burgesses from 1773 to 1789 and as a member of the state constitutional committee. According to family tradition, he was not pleased with the Republican form of government.

Subsequent to the War, Ridgely made his section a virtual pocket borough. It is said that he once gave an abundant feast to the powerful Methodist population in his district. Nothing like it had ever been seen locally. People flocked from far and near, and Ridgely was thenceforth the most popular man in the county.

Photograph by David McElroy

Hampton's servant bells.

Photograph by David McElroy

18

Hampton

In 1745 Charles Ridgely, Merchant, bought 1,500 acres in the wilderness of north central Baltimore County. The tract was called Northampton. To Northampton (roughly from Goucher College to the Loch Raven reservoir) he added adjoining pieces of Hampton Court and Oakhampton. Within five years the Ridgely holdings reached seven thousand acres. Though not adjacent, they included the present neighborhoods of Roland Park, Guilford, Blythewood, and Huntington.

The Merchant conveyed to his son Charles Ridgely, Builder, two thousand of these acres in 1760 and confirmed the gift at his death in 1772. To his grandson, John Robert Holliday, he left more land that would become Epsom.

During the Builder's life, Hampton established itself in three important economic areas. First, the Northampton grounds contained rich deposits of iron ore. Its furnaces supplied cannon and shot to the Continental forces during the War for Independence, and the iron made there was reputed to be some of the best in the world.

Second, Hampton had a quarry which supplied an excellent grade of limestone marble. From it the Ridgelys later donated stone for construction of the Towson Court House. And last, the estate embraced a large tobacco plantation at a time when sot-weed was the staple Maryland crop. In 1773-1774 the estate employed ninety-one servants (blacksmiths, gardeners, wagoners, coal miners, bakers, brickmakers, among others) exclusive of slaves.

An island of civilization, Hampton was surrounded by wilderness. It is said that during Hampton House's construction builders whose homes were some distance away stopped work at three o'clock each afternoon to avoid the wolves in the forest at night.

Charles Ridgely completed Hampton House in 1790, but died only six months after its completion. Because he and his wife Rebecca had no children, he left Hampton to his nephew and adopted son Charles Ridgely Carnan. To keep the Ridgely name from dying, the heir to Hampton changed his name to Charles Carnan Ridgely.

Apparently relations were tense between Carnan and Rebecca, and after a prolonged quarrel, the widow moved to Auburn, a smaller estate to the south.

It was Carnan who earmarked Hampton as a center of aristocratic social life in the early years of the nineteenth century. With fast horses in the stables and sleek spaniels in the kennels, he made a fashion of the fox hunt. Horse racing, music, large parties, and balls were *de rigueur* at Hampton.

The leisurely pattern of life continued, but its scale diminished as the century pressed on and many of the Ridgely acres were sold. The family's stay at Hampton lasted 158 years. The last members left in 1948 when the estate was bought by the Avalon Foundation and was shortly thereafter designated a national historic site.

Mrs. Charles Ridgely (Rebecca Dorsey) (1739-1812), wife of the Builder. The portraits of Charles and Rebecca by John Hesselius hang in Hampton's Great Hall.

Photograph by David McElroy

The drawing room. Its Empire furnishings are Ridgely family pieces.

Photograph by David McElroy

Though it had been designed for dining, this room was used by the Ridgelys as a sitting room and library. Its door allowed the children access to the grounds and therefore detoured muddy traffic from the Great Hall.

Photograph by David McElroy

The master bedroom. The canopied crib was that of John Ridgely, son of the Governor. The Governor's portable bathtub was perhaps made at Northampton iron furnace.

Above the fireplace is a picture of Priscilla, the Governor's wife. A Methodist, she had repeatedly refused to sit for such a worldly bauble as a portrait. So her husband hired an artist who, passing as his friend, made sketches of Priscilla without her knowledge during several visits. From the sketches he produced the portrait.

Photograph by David McElroy

The Great Hall. Used as a ballroom and state reception room, the hall seated fifty-one people comfortably at an 1820 dinner.

Photograph by David McElroy

A north window in the Great Hall. Early in Hampton's history, doors and shutters were barred shut at night in case of a slave uprising. At his death Charles Carnan Ridgely owned three hundred slaves.

Photograph by David McElroy

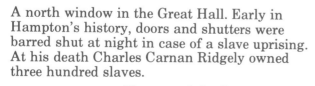

20

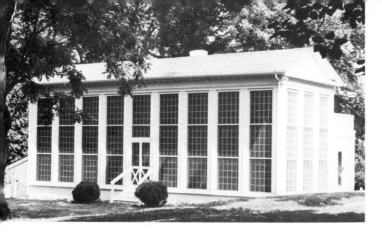

To keep fruit trees and flowers from freezing in winter, the Ridgelys built an orangery between 1829 and 1832. Its long windows faced south to allow the maximum of winter sunlight to reach through the narrow structure to the north wall, which blocked the wind.

The original orangery burned in 1928. Duplicating its Greek Revival style, the reconstruction was completed in 1976. It is rented for parties and receptions now.

Photograph by H. George Hahn

Charles Carnan Ridgely (1760-1829). Governor of Maryland from 1815-1818, Ridgely was said to have kept "the best table in America." Charles Carroll mentions a party at Hampton for which three hundred invitations were issued.

Photograph by David McElroy

"The Lady with the Harp" is Thomas Sully's portrait of Eliza Eichelberger Ridgely (1803-1867), daughter-in-law of the Governor. At her father's home in Baltimore, she is said to have played a harp for Lafayette on his last American visit in 1824.

Photograph by David McElroy

The northward view from the cupola. At his death, Charles Carnan Ridgely owned more than ten thousand acres in Baltimore County.

Photograph by David McElroy

A Local Cincinnatus

The War of 1812 raged over trade privileges as France and England bristled at the United States sea commerce that flourished while those nations warred. As they blockaded each other's ports, neutral American ships, many from Baltimore, slipped through to supply each country with needed wares. When England tried to abridge American rights in port and at sea, war was declared.

The local hero of that war was a son of Towsontown's first businessman. Nathan, the twelfth and last child of Ezekiel Towson, was born on January 22, 1784. An avid reader with but scant formal education, the boy seemed destined for a life at the family farm and tavern. In 1801, however, his rural life was interrupted by a trip south during which he joined the Natchez Volunteers. When he quelled a mass desertion attempt by the ill-treated volunteers, he was promoted to first lieutenant and soon rose to a captaincy in the Natchez Artillery.

His military life seemed finished when he returned to Towsontown to resume farming. But in 1807 he was appointed adjutant of the Seventh Maryland. When the war drums reached Towsontown in 1812 he was made a captain of artillery and drilled a unit of local boys on a two-acre field that held a federal powder magazine, later the foundation for the Epsom Chapel.

Legend has it that Towson was laying a barn floor when word of his commission arrived. On hearing the news, he drove home a spike, cast away his hammer, and said, "That is the last spike Nathan Towson will drive until he sends one into the touch-hole of the enemy's cannon."

Soon Towson and his Maryland Artillery were dispatched to Lake Erie, where the heaviest fighting was expected. There, Towson distinguished himself in four main actions. In the first, his guns repulsed the British attempt to recapture Fort Erie. During the battle his

An early oil portrait of Nathan Towson.

Courtesy of the Odd Fellows

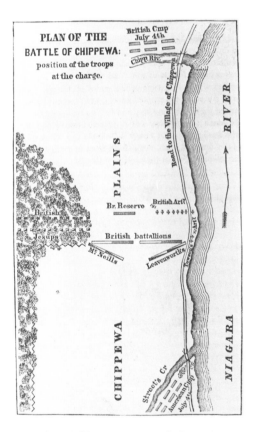

At the Battle of Chippewa on July 5, 1814, Towson's artillery on the shore of the Niagara River helped to give the American army its first victory following the disastrous defeat of 1813.

*From Mansfield's **Life of General Scott***

battery fired so rapidly that the British were turned back repeatedly.

At Chippewa his guns battered the British in an artillery duel, smashed their infantry assault, and virtually alone won the battle.

At Niagara, called by some historians the bloodiest action of the war, his guns fired from dawn to midnight without letup.

And at Bridgewater his guns fired on continually though both his lieutenants fell wounded and twenty-seven of his thirty-six men were killed or wounded.

Though Nathan Towson was praised by his commander, General Winfield Scott, higher praise was voiced by the British who named his battery "Towson's Lighthouse," for the constant glare of its gun flashes against the sky.

A man of great personal bravery, he commanded a boating party that captured two British brigs, the *Caledonia* and the *Detroit*, which he held though grounded in point-blank range of British cannon. The *Caledonia*

eventually became a vessel in Commodore Perry's victorious fleet. Nathan Towson also rode dauntlessly past a house occupied by the enemy who repeatedly fired at him. Later he discovered that one ball had ripped through his epaulette. He reflected that the British were not very good marksmen.

After the war the admiring citizens of Baltimore offered him the sheriffship of the city. When he refused, they presented him with a gold sword and named a street near Fort McHenry in his honor.

He was made Paymaster General of the Army in 1819. Serving throughout the Mexican War, he was breveted major-general in 1849. He died in Washington D. C., on July 25, 1854.

Mansfield's *Life of General Scott* records that the commander "galloped to our battery on the right, and called out to Towson—'Captain, more to the left; the enemy is there!' Towson on foot, and enveloped in smoke, could not see that the enemy's line had advanced inside the range of his last discharge. The gallant captain—than

whom no man in the army possessed a greater prowess—instantly changed the direction of his two remaining guns more to the left, and gave the final destructive fire, a second or two before the conflict of bayonets on that flank."

From Mansfield's Life of General Scott

Standing on what are now Goucher College grounds, the Epsom mansion was apparently a showplace. Built in the early 1800s, the house featured two glass-fronted conservatories that flanked a yellow front porch. Inside the front door was a dining room. Large windows like French doors opened out to admit a flood of light. That flood was filtered by a two-story portico on the left with Doric columns, probably added later. A few steps below the first floor were a breakfast room, pantry, and kitchen with fireplace and two brick ovens. Upstairs were the Chews' apartments, a nursery, and five other bedrooms.

Photograph courtesy of Towson Library, BCPL

Built in 1840, this house on Virginia Avenue was once part of the Epsom estate. The *Baltimore County American* of March 1, 1861, contained this advertisement for the house: "In Chewville adjoining Towson Town—Three Story Mansion on Virginia Avenue—hot, cold shower baths, water closets, cooking ranges, etc. and is admirably adapted for a female seminary or boarding house." The Chew and Grason families occupied the dwelling for many years. Originally it had a cupola.

Photograph by Carl Behm III

Epsom

When Governor Charles Carnan Ridgely gave his daughter Harriet in marriage, he gave her several hundred acres of the Ridgely property as dowry. Henry Banning Chew was the recipient of hand and land. After more land purchases, Henry and Harriet came to control some seven hundred acres. They named their estate Epsom, after Epsom Downs, the English racing town in Surrey, near which the Chew family held property.

This cannon once graced the lawn of Epsom. Of a type cast during the Revolutionary War, it had been mounted at the armory a short distance north of Joppa Road. After the armory was abandoned in the 1830s, Henry Chew brought the cannon to his home as an ornament.

Following the fire that destroyed Epsom, the cannon gradually settled into the ground. It was unearthed during excavation for the Julia Rodgers Library on the Goucher College campus in 1951.

Photograph courtesy of Goucher College

The gutted remains of Epsom House after the fire in 1886.

Photograph courtesy of Andrew Clemens

Mary Chew Grason Green as a young girl, probably in the 1890s.

Photograph courtesy of Frances Steuart Green

Chewville in 1975. Built by Benjamin Chew of Philadelphia in 1850, the stone house at the lower left is now a double private residence. Nestled in the trees beyond it is Peddlers' Village, a cluster of frame houses that have been converted into stores.

Photograph by Carl Behm III

Epsom Chapel: Mother of Towson Churches

On the Epsom grounds was an old building, said to have been a garrison during the eighteenth century. During the War of 1812, it was maintained as an ammunition magazine by the federal government. When Henry Banning Chew bought the property and its two acres in 1839, he donated them for church purposes, for at that time Towsonians had no church of their own. After the old magazine was razed, its stone was used to build a chapel twenty-six by forty feet. It stood on a little hill on Joppa Road near the east side of the present Hutzler's parking lot.

A "union" church, Epsom Chapel was open for use to any Evangelical minister or Christian denomination. Its first trustees included two Presbyterians, three Episcopalians, three Methodists, and a Baptist. After these denominations had founded their own churches, the chapel was used by the Boy Scouts as a meeting hall and by other congregations having no church building of their own. Epsom Chapel was razed in 1952.

Photograph by John W. McGrain

Glen Ellen

Another northern estate hewn from the vast Ridgely holdings was Glen Ellen. About 1830 Robert and William Gilmor bought a tract of two thousand acres along the Gunpowder River, land now part of the Loch Raven reservoir and watershed.

During an 1830 visit to Scotland, from which his grandfather had emigrated, Robert was the guest of Sir Walter Scott in his home, Abbotsford. Abbotsford's romantic beauty so impressed Gilmor that he commissioned the Gothic Revival architect A. J. Davis to design for him a home that would echo Abbotsford and rival Hampton.

Accordingly, Davis planned a castle that would loom five stories high with turret, moat, drawbridge, and mullioned windows in stone walls three feet thick. The massive structure, begun sometime between 1832 and 1835, was surrounded by wide lawns and sunken gardens, then fashionable in England. A forty-foot long drawing room, a dining room the width of the house, a huge ballroom, and some twenty-five bedrooms were features of Gilmor's lordly castle. Even its name was romantic, Glen Ellen, for Robert's wife Ellen Ward.

Suddenly, however, construction stopped. The second story was roofed and a wooden turret added. After expenses totaling seventy-five thousand dollars, Robert settled down in a truncated Glen Ellen with his wife and eleven children.

The Gilmor family held Glen Ellen through the War, during which six of its sons served the Confederate cause, two dying in service. Gilmor tenure lasted until Colonel Harry Gilmor sold the estate shortly before his death in 1883. Private ownership of the estate passed through several hands before Baltimore City bought much of it in 1912 and all of it by 1920 for the construction of Loch Raven reservoir. Thereafter, time, weather, and vandals ravished the castle, and finally wrecking crews put an end to it.

Photograph courtesy of Mildred S. Cassen

"A warm and mealy fragrance of the past" lingers in this photograph of a mill on the Gunpowder River. It was one of a number of mills that flourished between 1789, when the great flour boom began, and 1850, after which few large mills like this one were built. Between those years Ridgelys, Gilmors, Yellotts, Merrymans, and Morgans all owned mills in the area.

A country mill could be expected to produce about thirty-five barrels of flour per day, as Yellott's did in 1833. The miller received one-sixth of this yield.

Photograph by Charles W. E. Treadwell
Courtesy of Hilda N. Wilson

II. A Provincial Capital

At mid-century leisure and law were prominent new arrivals. To the south of Towson Baltimore businessmen built elegant summer mansions, and to the north two ministers planned a village of summer homes called Lutherville. At the same time occurred the event which assured Towson's importance: In 1854 it became the county seat. Thereafter, all roads in Baltimore County led to Towson.

The Southern Estates

Most of the land flanking York Road south of Susquehanna Avenue and down through Govans was once one thousand acres of wild country warranted by the King's Law Office to Job Evans in 1654. Evans named his property "Friend's Discovery." It was not until 1755 that William Govane bought the eastern five hundred acres, named them Drumquhasel after the Scottish home of his father near Glasgow. Later the name changed to Drumquhazel, then to Drumcastle.

The Govane plantation thrived there through the 1700s; not until the next century did the first phase of rapid development begin.

After Towsontown had been declared the

A 1915 map of the Southern estates.
From Bromley's **Atlas of Baltimore County**

Even as late as 1927, many estates were still intact. To the left of the York Road, the Dumbarton and Auburn estates dominate. To its right, Drumquhazel (in the York-Walker-Windwood Road wedge) and Wiltondale (above Stevenson Lane) remain farmland. Only Anneslie and Stoneleigh have begun their transformation into neighborhoods.

Photograph courtesy of Baltimore County

county seat in 1854, its businesses and professions began to thrive. The attraction of the pleasant, green land surrounding the town and the threat of cholera in Baltimore drew families beyond the city-county line at North Avenue (the boundary until 1919), first for summering, then for year-round living. Along the York Turnpike, Baltimore businessmen carved out elegant estates which chronicle the way of life of wealthy nineteenth-century Marylanders.

A horseman of the 1870s riding north on the York Turnpike from Govanstown would first pass the Drumquhazel estate on the east. Anneslie would next come into view, then the entrances to Dumbarton Farm and Stoneleigh. After passing these estates, he might stop at the forge of the Rodgers brothers, which was located where the lane leading to the Stevenson farms joined the Turnpike. Here a rider could rest while the blacksmith attended to his horse.

Beyond the Stevenson lane he would pass Auburn, then the smaller holdings of the Fisher, Gittings, and Taylor families to the west, and Aigburth Vale to the east. After coming to the stone house of the Bowen family (now the Tuxedo House, a short distance north of Burke Avenue), he entered Towsontown, beyond which lay the rich Chew, Ridgely, and Gilmor lands.

Looking north on York Road in 1946. The farmlands of 1927 have largely been plowed under to yield a crop of red brick houses. The row houses of Rodgers Forge stand on the left where the Dumbarton cows once grazed. And the small-plotted individual homes of the Anneslie and Stoneleigh neighborhoods on the right replace the estates after which they are named. The Drumquhazel estate at the center right stands mostly intact. Walker Avenue, then a dirt road, lies on its southern boundary.

Photograph courtesy of Cooper Walker

Looking north on York Road in 1976. The remaining meadows of 1946 are now foundations for shopping centers and churches. Where the Drumquhazel estate stood are now the Stewart's and Drumcastle shopping centers and the Drumcastle Apartments. On the left side of York Road are the A&P store, the York Road Plaza, WMAR-TV, and St. Pius X Church. Skyscrapers to the north jut up over Towson. The number of automobiles speaks volumes about the area's growth. Walker Avenue has been rebedded and repaved.

Photograph courtesy of Cooper Walker

Drumquhazel. The twenty-room house was made still more spacious when the south porch was enclosed for another dining room above which was built a sleeping porch in 1918. Though that was the year of the coldest winter in memory when the flu epidemic raged nationally, fresh air therapy was popular. Six of the Walkers slept on the porch throughout the year, warmed by "pigs," clay bottles filled with hot water, at their feet.

Photograph courtesy of Cooper Walker

Riding and fox hunting were staple adult activities. On the Drumquhazel grounds, at the Howard County Hunt, and in the Elkridge Hunt the Walkers rode hard. Robert H. Walker fox hunted at Howard County into his sixties on Warrior, a black horse that required a Hitchcock gag—a pulley device—because of his tough mouth. The animal served as hunter and farmhorse as well.

In this picture Walker and a guest stand where McCrory's 5 & 10 is now located.

Photograph courtesy of Cooper Walker

Drumquhazel: A Model of Country-House Life

In the 1840s the name Drumquhazel referred to a tract of some twenty-seven acres on which was built a three-story mansion. While the original owners are unknown, the first recorded occupant was George T. Sadtler, who held possession from 1869 to 1892.

In that year, for eighteen thousand dollars, ownership passed to Henry M. Walker (after whom Walker Avenue is named). Rider and huntsman, Mr. Walker claimed to have made a run to Howard and Monument Streets from Drumquhazel in twenty-one minutes to fetch a doctor for his wife, who was in labor. Equine eccentric as well, he rode into the Rennert Hotel to drink a toast of wine astride his mount. Noted equally as a party-giver, he once entertained over one thousand guests from three o'clock one afternoon until around noon the next day.

Less active leisure was the theme of the estate when Frank A. Furst, a German immigrant, Civil War veteran, and Baltimore political kingmaker (after whom Frankfurst Street in Baltimore is named), retired there for a year. Feeling isolated in the country, he returned to Baltimore City and pitched into business and political concerns.

After Elisha Walker, no kin of Henry, purchased the estate in 1901, life at Drumquhazel blended work and leisure. Indeed it may be seen as a model of country-house life for all the York Road estates.

Drumquhazel was a self-sustaining farm on which corn, cattle, hogs, chickens, pears, grapes, strawberries, apples, cherries, tomatoes, and asparagus flourished. In 1901 the farm methods were the same as those in the mid-nineteenth century. Mr. Walker's journal recounts meticulously the breeding of cattle, output of the farms, and prices for produce—corn at a penny an ear in 1903 was doubtless a bargain even then. And plowing, breeding, and fence-repairing occupied much of the farm-time. Cooper Walker, Elisha's grandson, well remembers the blood-curdling cries of hogs being slaughtered and the bizarre sight of headless chickens running amok after axing for the market. Because quail, rabbit, and squirrel were plentiful, small game, too, was fair game for the Walker table.

Leisure-time transformed the estate into a Currier and Ives world. Cooper Walker remembers winter scenes of sledding, skating on the ice pond, and tooling about the grounds in a one-horse open sleigh. Summer fun centered on the pond, where nude swimming and rafting provided out-of-school joys. One water game involved half-tipping a raft to decide a contest as to which boy could collect the most leeches on his legs. Picking strawberries and gathering chestnuts offered less chilling varieties of fun.

Though they stopped farming in the 1930s, the Walker family held the estate until 1948 when taxes rose and all expenses increased. Walker interest in the land has been kept intact, however. In 1948 the Drumcastle Apartment Corporation was formed and the spelling of the estate's name simplified. The project was completed under the Federal Housing Authority 608 Program. A lease of raw ground was negotiated with Associated Dry Goods for a Stewart & Co. branch store, completed in 1955. In 1959 the Walkers erected an office building on the southwest corner of the tract.

The parlor at Drumquhazel.

Photograph courtesy of Cooper Walker

Three generations. Seated are Lucy Cooper Walker (holding Katharine Wirt Walker) and Elisha Walker (holding Talbott Hunt Walker). Standing are the children's parents, Robert Hunt Walker and Amelia Himes Walker.

Photograph courtesy of Cooper Walker

Two children stop at play, entranced by the still of a summer afternoon. To the left is the Drumquhazel ice house which also included an herb room for the storage of potatoes, apples, and other perishables. In it was also a dairy filled with earthenware crocks. Ice kept the dairy cool.

Photograph courtesy of Cooper Walker

Amelia Himes Walker (1880-1974) of Drumquhazel at age eighteen. In 1917 this Towsonian picketed the White House in protest of President Wilson's anti-suffragist policies. For her protest she was imprisoned with fifteen other women. Disdaining the twenty-five dollar fine, she accepted instead a sixty-day sentence in Occoquan, the District of Columbia workhouse. A newspaper interview with Mrs. Walker describing jail conditions helped trigger nationwide prison reform. With other imprisoned suffragists, Mrs. Walker proudly wore an iron pin in the shape of chained jail doors. During Wilson's second term, Drumquhazel was filled with flags and banners advocating "Equal Rights" and "Votes for Women." In 1919 she made a coast-to-coast speaking tour on the "Prison Special" to canvass for the last two senatorial votes needed to pass the nineteenth amendment. It was enacted the next year.

During the teens and twenties, she made Drumquhazel a salon for the arts. In the late 1930s she ran for the Maryland House of Delegates. Though defeated, she won enough votes to collect a ten dollar wager from Harrison Rider, the influential Baltimore County political boss. She also served as Chairman of the National Woman's Party.

Photograph courtesy of Cooper Walker

Lucy Cooper Walker and unidentified child ready for a ride.

Photograph courtesy of Cooper Walker

Robert Hunt Walker helps his wife Amelia from the sleigh after a ride in a 1938 snow storm.

Photograph courtesy of Cooper Walker

Looking southwest, one sees Walker Avenue and the corn shocks lying to the south. To the right is the ice pond. Note the ramp up which ice slabs were slid onto wagons.

Walker Avenue was named for Henry M. Walker, who started the road in 1895 with a donation of land to the county and completed it with one thousand dollars of his own money. His reason was to provide a short cut between York and Hillen Roads which would save two miles of travel over Regester Avenue.

Photograph courtesy of Cooper Walker

Photograph courtesy of Cooper Walker

35

Anneslie

Photograph by Carl Behm III

Anneslie was built in 1855. Surrounded by groves of great trees and meadows, the house was a showplace of nineteenth-century elegance. Its original owner, Frederick Harrison, used Anneslie as his summer home. His daughter married Lennox Birckhead, and the house remained in the Birckhead family until 1972. Although many had feared that this fifteen-room Italian-Revival mansion might be razed for a housing development, it was sold for fifty-two thousand dollars to a private owner.

A 1916 plan of the estate shows Anneslie to be a working farm of ninety-eight acres with hog pens, orchards, and two ice ponds, as well as a tennis court and a boxwood garden.

In 1921 Charles Steffey purchased all but three acres of the land for a housing development. He built a number of homes in the new neighborhood before buyers had been found. Though common now, such an approach was unusual in 1921.

Frederick Harrison, a West Point graduate, was a United States Assistant Civil Engineer in Washington, D. C. He surveyed the B & O Railroad to the Ohio River, the Michigan and Illinois Canal, and the Northern Central Railroad as far as Cockeysville. He died in 1871 at age eighty-eight.

From Sharf's **History of Baltimore City and County**

Lennox Birckhead, a Union veteran of the Civil War, married Anne Harrison. He was the first of the Birckheads to occupy Anneslie. This picture was taken in 1883.

Photograph courtesy of Taylor A. Birckhead

A party at Anneslie before a fox hunt in 1893.
Photograph courtesy of J. Rieman McIntosh

Stoneleigh

Just north of Anneslie and south of Stevenson Lane stood Stoneleigh. It was built between 1849 and 1852 as the summer house of Robert P. Brown, a wealthy Baltimore importer whose brother-in-law, Frederick Harrison, lived at neighboring Anneslie. Its final cost—with a tenant house—was $17,381.94.

Considered a showplace in its day, the house was named for Stoneleigh Abbey, a place that Brown was taken with during a journey in the British Isles.

With an exterior of brick, stucco, and white pine woodwork, Stoneleigh's composition is a lost art. The house rose to a height of two deep stories with an attic. Its many stained-glass windows, breaks, gables, and small towers marked it as peculiarly mid-Victorian American.

The original estate totalled 130 acres, with a long, shaded driveway, now Stoneleigh Road, leading east from the York Turnpike. All but nineteen acres were divided into lots for the development of the neighborhood Stoneleigh in the 1920s. The mansion itself was demolished in 1955 and its grounds cut up into plots for another seventy-seven homes.

Photograph courtesy of J. Hollis Albert, Jr.

The Victorian Age was a time of ornament and upholstery, as these rooms in Stoneleigh mansion show.

Photographs courtesy of J. Hollis Albert, Jr.

In 1930 Stoneleigh School was built to serve the new neighborhoods south of Towson.

Photograph by Carl Behm III

The large pond that supplied the Stoneleigh estate with ice is now the site of the Stoneleigh community swimming pool.

Photograph by Carl Behm III

REAR VIEW.

THE BARN.

Courtesy of J. Rieman McIntosh

Joseph Henry Rieman (1822-1897) was an industrialist, banker, and official of the Northern Central and B & O Railroads. An ardent horticulturist as well, Rieman entered into a friendly rivalry with a county neighbor to determine who could landscape his estate with the most exotic trees and shrubs. The cedar of Lebanon that he planted, a prize example of its species, was the largest in the east until it was pulled down in a 1963 snow storm.

Photograph courtesy of J. Rieman McIntosh

Dumbarton Farm

In 1854 Robert A. Taylor built an elegant mansion off the west side of York Road, about a mile and a half south of Towsontown. He lived in this house of Greek Revival design, then highly fashionable, for ten years before selling it with 180 acres to Joseph H. Rieman of Baltimore, who made it his summer home. Rieman purchased Dumbarton Farm for sixty-five thousand dollars. His ledger details the terms of the transaction: $7,000 in gold, 3,900 pounds sterling, and $19.44 in cash.

Rieman operated Dumbarton as a working farm. One of the first to import the Jersey breed into Maryland, he brought the sixteen-year-old bull, Sir Davey, from the Isle of Jersey in the 1860s. Soon Rieman's herd of registered Jerseys became well known on the show circuit.

When Rieman died in 1897, Dumbarton Farm went into his estate. In the mid-1920s Rieman's son Charles cut through and named Dumbarton Road. Shortly thereafter most of the estate was sold and construction of the Rodgers Forge row-house development began.

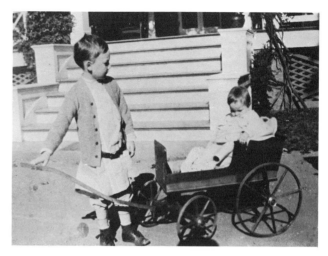

Children play in front of Dumbarton house.
Photograph courtesy of J. Rieman McIntosh

Because provision was made for the caretaker of Dumbarton Farm to remain in his home during his lifetime, this small house still stands. It is now surrounded by the playing fields of Dumbarton Junior High School, not farmland.

Although one may find some solace in the preservation of the Dumbarton mansion by the Baltimore County Board of Education, one must also heed the implications of the way in which it was acquired: The house was sold to the county under threat of condemnation.

Now the interior has been converted into offices, the front steps have been removed from the porch, and the white paint appropriate to the Greek Revival architectural mode has been stripped away.

Photograph courtesy of J. Rieman McIntosh

Joseph Rieman's son, Charles, in a carriage in front of Farm Gates about 1912. After his father's death, Charles Rieman took over management of the farm. Under him, the Dumbarton Jersey herd was continued with great success. It won many championships at the State Fair at Timonium and produced the milk which was one of Dumbarton Farm's principal products.

Photograph courtesy of J. Rieman McIntosh

41

By World War I Rieman's daughter, Charlotte, and her husband, David Gregg McIntosh, were summering in the white mansion house at Dumbarton. When the Rieman estate was broken up in 1924, Mrs. McIntosh purchased the house and twenty-six acres. Dumbarton remained her home for the next thirty years.

Photograph courtesy of J. Rieman McIntosh

David Gregg McIntosh, Jr. (1877-1940). Like his father, McIntosh was a lawyer with offices in Towson. He was a member of the Maryland House of Delegates from 1913-1919. Beginning in 1920, he served four terms in the State Senate. In 1924, 1927, and 1929, he was its president.

Photograph courtesy of J. Rieman McIntosh

Although the present Board of Education building is the house which most Towsonians associate with Dumbarton, there was a second brick house already on the property when Taylor purchased it in 1854. For a time the home of Charles E. Rieman, it was torn down when James Keelty began the construction of Rodgers Forge.

The house, which faced west, was known as Farm Gates. It was in the center of the Rieman property, near the present intersection of Pinehurst and Murdock Roads. The drive on the right wound from the Bellona Avenue entrance to Farm Gates and then north to Dumbarton House.

Photograph courtesy of J. Rieman McIntosh

A one-horse power lawn mower.

Photograph courtesy of J. Rieman McIntosh

Rodgers Forge

The Forge is shown here in a 1920s photograph.

Photograph courtesy of Robert Cardwell

Other businesses thrived on the horse-and-buggy traffic.

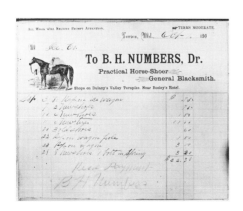

It was 1800 when a nineteen-year-old Irish immigrant, George Rodgers, bought four acres from the sprawling estate of Govane Howard. Rodgers set up a blacksmith and cartwright business facing the York Turnpike at the southeast corner of Stevenson's lane. There the horse-shoeing business passed through four generations of his family. By 1891 the family land had expanded to ten acres.

Well into this century the Rodgers forge served the stud farm at Wiltondale, the estates nearby, and the fox hunting set at Elkridge. Also housing a tiny post office from 1891 to 1931, it was the hub of local life. But its day had passed even before it burned in 1946. Just as the estates around it had been parceled into housing developments, the blacksmith shop would have had to surrender eventually to a gasoline station.

Now Rodgers Forge lives on in the name of the quiet colonial row-house community built on the land that had been the Dumbarton estate. Begun in 1932, the neighborhood contains 1,777 red brick homes in which some seven thousand people dwell. It was constructed by James Keelty and Sons.

The older row homes of Rodgers Forge, with their well-kept yards, flower beds, and neat, simple lines suggest a touch of English village life. Unlike other row-house communities, the architectural variety includes designs from the Tudor to the sloped-gabled "humble" style of the eighteenth century.

Perhaps one reason that modern Towsonians and Baltimoreans are so unflappable is the row house. Close living conditions, parking problems, and the Saturday-night parties that everyone experiences (actively and passively) promote tolerance by traditional conditioning.

Photograph by Carl Behm III

A 1900 view of Auburn.
Photograph courtesy of Towson State University

Henry Chrystie Turnbull
Photograph courtesy of Towson State University

A library at Auburn in 1946.
Photograph courtesy of Towson State University

Auburn

A family quarrel began the history of Auburn house. When Charles Ridgely, Builder, died, his estate was divided among four nephews, largely according to the old Law of Entailment, which family custom still observed. The principal heir was Charles Carnan, Ridgely's nephew and adopted son. Soon Carnan and Rebecca Dorsey, Ridgely's widow, developed an antagonism over his treating her "with the Greatest Disrespect and Slights." For the surrender of all further claim to her late husband's property at Hampton, the widow received from her nephew a tract of 244¼ acres off the York Turnpike originally called Demitt's Delight.

Carnan had patented the land in 1790. Shortly thereafter, Auburn, conceived as a smaller version of Hampton, was built. Tucked into the rolling green hills, the mansion of some fourteen rooms with verandas at front, side, and rear evinces the spacious leisure of the eighteenth-century country house. There

Rebecca lived until her death in 1812.

After 1816 John Yellott and then Benjamin Moore owned the house before Henry Chrystie Turnbull bought it in 1836. Tragically, Auburn was destroyed by fire thirteen years later. Turnbull rebuilt the mansion and the family held it until 1913. In that year Auburn was sold to John Fife Symington, who changed its name to Kenoway House. Deeded to Sheppard-Pratt Hospital in 1944, the house was the residence of Dr. Harry Murdock, medical director of the hospital and the last person to live at Auburn. In 1971 Towson State University purchased the property.

Restored in 1976 as a dining club, the historic home brings together faculty and alumni of the university as well as members of the professional and mercantile communities. Not a static museum, the Towson Club affords people the opportunity to gather in an atmosphere befitting Auburn's dignified past.

White walls and floor-to-ceiling windows brighten the dining room at Auburn. The airy, high-ceilinged room reveals the first principle of early American air-conditioning: Hot air rises.

Photograph courtesy of Towson State University

Auburn, summer 1977: Towson State University vice president Joseph Cox, vice president Paul Wisdom, president James Fisher, and vice president Wayne Schelle.

Photograph courtesy of Towson State University
Inset photograph by Carl Behm III

Fire and Folly: Two main catastrophes have befallen Auburn House in its 186 years. The first occurred during the height of a fall storm in 1849 when fire destroyed the building beyond repair. Only three eighteenth-century doors survived the holocaust.

The second disaster is recent. From about 1965 to 1974, the house was plagued by vandals both wanton and designing. Both the brainless smashing of windows and other appointments and the calculated theft of black Italian marble mantlepieces and heavy Victorian doors dramatize the need for vigilant concern for old buildings. The vandalism of time has had its way as well. This destruction, at the cost of tens of thousands of dollars, offers evidence that American public consciousness is often an absentee landlord of the past.

Photograph courtesy of Towson State University

Auburn shows the influence of the eighteenth-century English ethic in its symmetry, soft colors, and dignified strength. These qualities were retained when the mansion was rebuilt in the 1850s although the influence of the Italianate and Federal styles, then popular, may be observed. In 1915 John Fife Symington added the service wing on the left.

The Bride and Groom, the two trees that shelter the front, or south, entrance are said to be the oldest English elms in Maryland. A ring count dates them to 1789.

On March 17, 1975 Auburn was received into the National Register of Historic Places.

Photograph courtesy of Towson State University

Zelda Fitzgerald wrote of La Paix: "We have a soft shady place here that's like a paintless playhouse abandoned when the family grew up. It's surrounded by apologetic trees and warning meadows and creaking insects." Above the front door was a sign reading *Pax Vobiscum.*

Photograph by John W. McGrain

F. Scott Fitzgerald (1896-1940), probably at his desk at La Paix. In less meditative moments, the author annoyed many Towsonians by racing his noisy Stutz Bearcat up and down York Road, kicking up dust and frightening grazing animals.

Photograph courtesy of **The Sunpapers**

La Paix

Above Rodgers forge, between Auburn and York Road, stood a home built by the Turnbull family in 1885 as a summer house. Even before its most famous resident arrived, La Paix had a literary tradition of its own. There a Turnbull scion had edited the magazine, *The New Eclectic,* and a Turnbull matron had written historical romances. And the Southern poet, Sidney Lanier, who stayed at the family's home in Baltimore, had no doubt visited the twenty-eight-acre place.

But for eighteen months in 1932 and 1933, La Paix was the rented home of the Lion of the Jazz Age, F. Scott Fitzgerald. Much of his best work behind him, he had come to Towson during his wife's stays at Johns Hopkins' Phipps' Clinic and later at Sheppard-Pratt Hospital.

During his first year there, Fitzgerald cavorted in white flannels on the tennis court, tossed a football with young Andrew Turnbull, and did card tricks for his daughter and the Turnbull children. Fitzgerald and T. S. Eliot, in Baltimore for lectures sponsored by the Turnbulls, took country walks and discussed the state of literature. H. L. Mencken and John Dos Passos visited as well. After dark, a lamp burned late in Fitzgerald's second story bedroom as he completed writing *Tender Is the Night.*

While at La Paix Fitzgerald battled alcoholism, his wife's illness, mild tuberculosis, as well as insomnia, loneliness, financial problems, and the acute sense that he had lost his creative powers. That his stories were not selling underlined his problems. Of his wife's hospitalization he said, "I left my capacity for hoping on the little roads that led to Zelda's sanatariums."

Like the novelist, the house was in eclipse. During the Fitzgerald year and a half, La Paix was a damp, drafty Victorian pile, long out of fashion, its elegance only a distant echo.

To make way for a St. Joseph Hospital parking lot, La Paix was demolished in 1961, a victim of civilized vandalism.

Young Andrew Turnbull and Scottie, Fitzgerald's daughter, at La Paix in 1932.

Later a biographer of Fitzgerald and Thomas Wolfe, Turnbull was a professor of history and literature at Harvard and Brown Universities. To him Fitzgerald was a companion during the Towson period and a correspondent afterwards. Turnbull died in 1970.

Photograph courtesy of Mrs. Jerome Kidder

47

The Aigburth mansion.

Photograph by John W. McGrain

Aigburth Vale

In 1853 the distinguished English-born actor John E. Owens bought Rock Spring Farm, some 198 acres south of Towsontown. Changing the name to Aigburth Vale, Owens built the mansion where he lived with his wife, Mary C. Stevens, for thirty-four years. He transformed the original farm into one of the most beautiful estates in Baltimore County.

Making theatrical appearances in Europe and the United States, Owens achieved great fame—and great wealth. He was once acknowledged to be the wealthiest actor in America. His fortune enabled him to improve his estate and gardens and to fill Aigburth with rich furniture, paintings, engravings, and many books. Perhaps his success reconciled his father-in-law, a Baltimore Methodist merchant, to his daughter's marriage to an actor.

After Owens' death, Aigburth was used by city residents as a summer home during the 1890s. In 1919 Dr. George Sargent established a hospital for adults there. And in 1950 the Baltimore County School Board signed a long-term lease to use Aigburth Vale for administrative offices.

Built around 1860 by Jacob Reese, this home was once the gatehouse for Aigburth Vale. It stands at York Road and Cedar Avenue.

Photograph by Carl Behm III

The original farmhouse. Owens often made his farming ability the butt of his comedy. While showing off Aigburth Vale to his friends, Owens usually remarked, "Delightful? Yes. But revenue? No. Honestly I tell you that if it were not for John Owens the actor, John Owens the farmer would starve." As his wife remembered,

"When his friends call, he sets out milk and champagne, with the tearful request that they will take the champagne because it doesn't cost as much."

From Mary Stevens Owens'
Memories of John E. Owens

John E. Owens (1823-1886) rose to fame as a leading actor and theater manager. The theme of his success was his ability to please people.

One of Owens' antics illustrates his sense of audience—and his celebrity. Due in Terre Haute, Indiana, for a show at 7:30 p.m., he was delayed in Indianapolis, seventy-eight miles away. He telegraphed the theater manager, who replied, "The audience will wait for you." At every succeeding train station the two exchanged similar messages, the manager announcing periodically to the waiting audience that Owens was seventy miles away, then fifty, then thirty, and so on. Reaching Terre Haute, Owens dashed to the theater, dressed quickly, and stepped on stage at 11 p.m. to a deafening roar of welcome. When the curtain fell at 2 a.m., the crowd dispersed in a merry mood. A poem entitled "Owens' Ride" in the Cincinnati *Enquirer* commemorated the event.

Warmly praised by Charles Dickens in 1865, Owens is considered to have been the best American comedian of his day.

From Mary Stevens Owens'
Memories of John E. Owens

Land for a Courthouse

In 1853 Towson was campaigning hard to become the Baltimore County seat. Prominent Towson landholders each offered to donate five acres for the Court House and Jail. One of these, Grafton M. Bosley, had inherited an estate from his uncle, Josiah Marsh, in 1850. Bosley had already donated land for the Odd Fellows' Hall on York Road, and it was his property that was selected for the official buildings.

A physician, Bosley later left medical practice to administer his lands.

Bosley built his home in 1860 at what is now Georgia Court. In 1929 the house and fourteen acres became the Presbyterian Home of Maryland.

The human scale of the 1854 Court House and the dignity of its landscaping contrast sharply with the colossus of the 1976 courts building.

Photograph courtesy of John E. Raine, Jr.

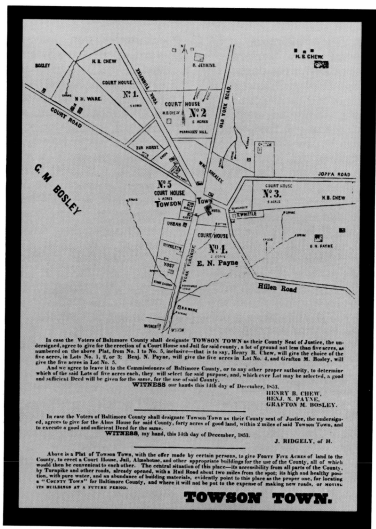

In case the Voters of Baltimore County shall designate TOWSON TOWN as their County Seat of Justice, the undersigned, agree to give for the erection of a Court House and Jail for said county, a lot of ground not less than five acres, as numbered on the above Plat, from No. 1 to No. 5, inclusive—that is to say, Henry B. Chew, will give the choice of the five acres, in Lots No. 1, 2, or 3; Benj. N. Payne, will give the five acres in Lot No. 4, and Grafton M. Bosley, will give the five acres in Lot No. 5.

And we agree to leave it to the Commissioners of Baltimore County, or to any other proper authority, to determine which of the said Lots of five acres each, they will select for said purpose, and, which ever Lot may be selected, a good and sufficient Deed will be given for the same, for the use of said County.

WITNESS our hands this 14th day of December, 1853.
HENRY B. CHEW,
BENJ. N. PAYNE,
GRAFTON M. BOSLEY.

In case the Voters of Baltimore County shall designate Towson Town as their County seat of Justice, the undersigned, agrees to give for the Alms House for said County, forty acres of good land, within 2 miles of said Towson Town, and to execute a good and sufficient Deed for the same.

WITNESS, my hand, this 14th day of December, 1853.
J. RIDGELY, of H.

Above is a Plat of Towson Town, with the offer made by certain persons, to give FORTY FIVE ACRES of land to the County, to erect a Court House, Jail, Almshouse, and other appropriate buildings for the use of the County, all of which would then be convenient to each other. The central situation of this place—its accessibility from all parts of the County, by Turnpike and other roads, already opened, with a Rail Road about two miles from the spot; its high and healthy position, with pure water, and an abundance of building materials, evidently point to this place as the proper one, for locating a "COUNTY TOWN" for Baltimore County, and where it will not be put to the expense of making new roads, or MOVING ITS BUILDINGS AT A FUTURE PERIOD.

TOWSON TOWN.

This 1853 plat shows the five parcels of land offered to the county by Henry B. Chew, Benjamin N. Payne, and Grafton M. Bosley.

Courtesy of Towson Library, BCPL

The Presbyterian Home of Maryland, formerly the Bosley mansion.

Photograph by Carl Behm III

51

Sot-Weed to Clippers to Farm Wagons: The Flag Follows Trade

The lineage of the Towson Court House is rooted deep in the woods of seventeenth-century north central Maryland. Then Baltimore County included all of what is now Harford, Carroll, and Cecil Counties and large parts of the present Anne Arundel, Frederick, and Kent Counties. The population of old Baltimore County in 1659, when it was founded, was probably fewer than two thousand; that of all of the Maryland Colony was but twelve thousand. And with such a residence spread, justice was *ad hoc* if not homespun, as judges held court in their own homes while dogs barked, infants cried, and pies baked.

The first courthouse was erected in 1674 at Old Baltimore on the Bush River, a place easily accessible by water and near tobacco country. When the dormer-windowed log courthouse fell into disrepair, it was sold for four thousand pounds of tobacco. A new site was chosen on the banks of the Gunpowder, again near the tobacco fields as the law traveled with the staple crop. Its courthouse was in use by 1697 or 1698.

But by 1712, when the southern and western parts of old Baltimore County had attracted more settlers, the seat was removed to the town of Joppa. Because of its excellent harbor, the British government declared it a port of entry, an official place where planters loaded crops—especially tobacco—for the European and Indies trade. Warehouses, wharves, shipyards, and customs hummed with business. Racetracks, salesmen, tobacco planters, and inns prospered in this vital town that offered a ten percent discount on all debts paid in tobacco. For half a century Joppa was the most important town in old Baltimore County.

Free trade insisted on rigid law. The courthouse and the prison with its pillory, stocks, and whipping post stood as clear reminders that to violate property was to disrupt civil order. The gallows loomed nearby, the last word in eighteenth-century justice, in which theft could be a capital offense.

As tobacco stores bulged and tobacco prices fell, Joppa's importance diminished. Fewer ships sailed into and out of the harbor, customs suffered, and silt soon filled the channel. As residents moved away, swamplands spread and malaria swept in. More people moved. Houses were cannibalized for repair wood and fuel. Soon all signs of life disappeared. Even the dead in St. John's Churchyard were removed to Kingsville. A county seat had fallen victim to the inexorable laws of trade. The year Towson was born, Joppa died.

Meanwhile, Baltimore on the Patapsco had been growing since 1728, its large, deep harbor attracting greater tonnage because of a greater variety of exports. Owing to the port's new commercial and maritime dignity, a large number of citizens petitioned the General Assembly that Joppa be abandoned as county seat and that a new courthouse be built in Baltimore City. The petition granted, the city's (and county's) first courthouse rose in 1771 on Calvert Street near Jones Falls. In 1809 and 1835 still new and larger courthouses were built to accommodate the swelling dockets and other records.

As the port grew, it developed priorities far different from those of the rest of Baltimore County. Street lighting, a water system, and police protection became necessities that countians outside the port's limits were reluctant to be taxed for. Moreover, the north countians wanted a more speedy administration of justice with a courthouse not so far south.

Since the first case was tried there in 1857, little has changed in what is now Courtroom No. 5. Around the room was a garden of spittoons, targets of incredibly accurate aim. Until 1958, prisoners quaked in a bull pen in the courtroom itself and heard verdicts and sentences pronounced on luckless miscreants. Often courtroom spectators would loudly condemn a state's attorney for failing to get a conviction. The walls are hung with oil paintings of famous judges, attorneys, and state's attorneys. When the old Court House was remodeled for county offices, Towson's first courtroom was not altered. Appropriately, it will be reserved for special trials in the future.

Painting by T. Scott Offutt

Accordingly, Baltimore City was separated from Baltimore County in 1851 by act of the General Assembly. And if each would have a separate government, the new county needed a seat.

Until 1853 county seats had been designated by the General Assembly, but now that body allowed Baltimore County to select a seat by popular ballot. Various local interests campaigned, and on the third ballot of February 13, 1854, Towsontown was selected.

Great jubilation abounded in Towsontown and a grand illumination capped the event. The old frame tavern of Henry Banning Chew atop Sater Hill was set afire to commemorate the occasion.

The Court House, still in use, was built on five acres donated by Dr. Grafton N. Bosley. Stone was donated by the Ridgelys. For thirty-thousand dollars the two-story structure was built by William H. Allen to the architectural plans of Thomas and James Dixon.

Several times during its early years the Court House was threatened by destruction. In 1861 an attempt was made to burn it; though the building was saved, the civil dockets and some clerk's papers were lost. In 1864 Towsonians feared retaliation on the Court House by the Confederate raider Harry Gilmor for Union destruction in the South, but it was not molested. And on a stormy midnight of 1867, three masked bandits overpowered the watchman and blasted the iron safe. The thirteen thousand dollars in cash and bonds they escaped with were private funds, however, left by citizens in the hopeful safety of the iron vault.

An advertisement in the *Baltimore County Advocate* of December 1859.

Many of the residences close to the Court House have been converted into lawyers' offices.

Photograph by Carl Behm III

The gallows in the jail yard. *The Jeffersonian* of 1954 reported that when hangings were still public in Towson, "they took place at daybreak, and the curious spent the preceding night in Court House Square. Drugstores stayed open all night to sell sandwiches to the crowd."

Once a hanging was delayed until ten o'clock. Because they would be late for work, many spectators berated the tardy victim and his executioner. "Children on their way to school passed by as the unfortunate condemned man dangled at the end of a rope."

Photograph by Charles W. E. Treadwell
Courtesy of Hilda N. Wilson

The Towson jail was built at the same time as the Court House.

Photograph by Carl Behm III

Spanish Spoils and German Spies

The five-ton cannon that guards Court House Square is a prize of the Spanish-American War. It was captured at Manila Bay on May 1, 1898, by Admiral Dewey and awarded by him to a Towsonian who had served with valor during the battle. Aptly, its base is emblazoned with such spirited martial utterings as Schley's "There is glory enough for all" and Dewey's "You may fire, Gridley, when you are ready."

Amid the great stir of gathered villagers on a May afternoon of 1903, the gun was hauled into the square from the Baltimore City docks on the largest of Towson's wagons. From his fee of thirty-five dollars, Harry Groom, the ice man, paid out fifty cents and a drink of potato liquor to each of his thirty-five sturdy helpers. The portage took five hours, plus the time when the overloaded vehicle was bogged down to its hubcaps in the square's lawn. A staunch adversary to the last, the Spanish coastal gun had sunk the flagship of Towsontown's ice-wagon fleet.

Photograph by Carl Behm III

The Northern Central Railroad

The tracks of the Northern Central pass to the west of Towson. Once they formed a vital link in the Pennsylvania Railroad's mainline from Washington and Baltimore to Harrisburg and the west. Then the Northern Central's famous train, the *Liberty Limited,* would roar by the stations at Ruxton, Riderwood, and Lutherville.

The immediate ancestor of the Northern Central, the Baltimore & Susquehanna Railroad, was chartered in 1828. Its founders hoped to encourage trade between Baltimore and southern Pennsylvania, a goal which raised opposition in the Pennsylvania legislature. While the southern Pennsylvania interests supported the plan enthusiastically, Philadelphians, fearing their port would suffer as a result of a rail route to the closer seaport at Baltimore, lobbied against it.

Construction at the Baltimore end of the line began in August 1829. On July 4, 1831, horse-drawn cars inaugurated service from the Belvedere Street Depot, which was several blocks east of the location of the present Pennsylvania Station, to Relay House, a station

A southbound local passenger train stops at the Ruxton Station in 1904. The forerunner of this stone building was constructed in 1885, and its presence influenced the development of a neighborhood of summer homes on what had been the Heiser farm. The most famous of these Ruxton residences was that of William Pinkney Whyte, whose long political career included the offices of Mayor of Baltimore, Governor of Maryland, and United States Senator.

Mrs. Elsie T. Potts, station agent and postmistress who lived in the building from 1935 to 1960, recalled the warm fraternity of "workers, clerkers, and shirkers" who waited at the station every morning bound for jobs and shopping in Baltimore. Around the station were a memorial oak, planted for the local dead of World War I, a forsythia planted by the Ruxton Club, a hawthorn, called "The Birds' Hotel," and a tall fir, decorated for the holidays in December. The warm and cheerful station was a hub of communal life in a Christmas garden world.

The station was destroyed—with the memorial oak—in 1963 for two apartment buildings.

Photograph courtesy of Herbert H. Harwood

at Lake Roland. When the Pennsylvania legislature finally approved the founding of the York & Maryland Line Railroad Company in 1832, the Baltimore & Susquehanna expanded northward to connect with it. The line was opened to Timonium in September 1832, and the railroad acquired its first steam locomotive, the *Herald*, built in England by George Stephenson. Track between Baltimore and York was completed in 1838.

The two decades prior to the Civil War were ones of growth and consolidation. In 1846 the incorporation of the York & Cumberland Railroad Company established a mainline from Baltimore to Harrisburg, with connections to the rich Cumberland Valley. In 1849 the Calvert Street Station opened; on the site of the present *Sunpapers* building, the station served the railroad for more than one hundred years. Finally, in 1854, the Baltimore & Susquehanna merged with its three principal connecting railroads to form the Northern Central Railroad. The Pennsylvania Railroad acquired a controlling interest in the Northern Central seven years later.

When the railroad completed laying track to Sunbury, Pennsylvania, in 1858, the Northern Central had a mainline of 138 miles. Its significance cannot be overestimated. The Northern Central made Baltimore the closest seaport to Lake Erie and opened the city to the coal fields in the Lykens and Shamokin valleys.

The heyday of the Northern Central has ended. The *Liberty Limited*, which first carried passengers in 1923, made its last run in 1957. When the Northern Central had become one of the earliest victims of the Civil War, the bridges that had been burned to prevent Union soldiers from moving south were immediately rebuilt by a nation that needed railroads. In contrast, when several bridges in northern Baltimore County washed out during Hurricane Agnes in 1972, the death knell sounded for through service on the Northern Central line. The bridges have not been replaced and probably will not be. Perhaps local commuter service will resurrect the Northern Central. For now, however, weeds grow in the ballast and the rails rust.

When two Lutheran ministers, Dr. John Gottleib Morris and Dr. Benjamin Kurtz, searched for a suitable tract of land on which to build a seminary for women, the Northern Central Railroad undoubtedly loomed large in their minds. The success of their venture depended on comfortable and reasonably rapid access to Baltimore. For what Morris and Kurtz had determined to do was no less than to underwrite the cost of their college through the sale of building lots for a community of summer homes.

In 1852 the ministers' dream began to take tangible form when they purchased a large tract of farmland on the Northern Central line less than two miles north of the Towson Court House. They named the future village after Martin Luther, the sixteenth-century father of the Lutheran Church.

Two of the first buildings completed in Lutherville symbolize the ministers' blending of religious purposefulness and secular practicality. The Lutheran faith was made the literal hub of the village, for surveyors laid out roads which radiated from St. Paul's Evangelical Lutheran Church. Yet the construction of the Lutherville Station on the Northern Central Railroad was as crucial to the fulfilment of the ministers' dream as was the building of the church. On the roads of Lutherville the village planners platted 118 building lots. The Northern Central Railroad made them saleable by enabling businessmen to summer in the village and commute to the city.

The plan worked. The cool greenery of the countryside drew Baltimoreans from the hot brick and concrete of the city. The construction of Landon House, a summer hotel, provided the additional inducements of playing fields, concerts, art exhibitions, bowling, and picnic groves. Income from the sale of the building lots enabled the ministers to open the Lutherville Female Seminary to students on October 2, 1854.

The Seminary was the special dream of Dr. Morris, who oversaw its operation until the 1890s. He considered the Seminary the sister institution to Gettysburg College, and he was justly proud of the college's economic independence, which made it unnecessary for him to ask any financial assistance of the Lutheran Church.

The first twenty-five to thirty students of the Seminary met a faculty of nine instructors, five of whom were women. And they faced a rigorous curriculum. One commentator on the history of the Seminary has cited as evidence of its scholarly intentions the establishment of an astronomical observatory in the tower of the college building, and she speculates that this may have been the first observatory built for "feminine stargazers."

In 1895 the college was re-established under a new charter, which terminated its connections with the Lutheran Church and with Dr. Morris. The Lutherville Female Seminary became the Maryland College for Young Ladies and School of Music, later the Maryland College for Women. The new charter provided the institution with full collegiate powers and authorized it to bestow the degrees of Bachelor of Arts, Bachelor of Science, and Bachelor of Literature on its graduates.

Despite the gentility of its name, the Maryland College for Young Ladies was not without a radical element—or at least one daring young woman. In 1911 the principal college building was burned to the ground, all because one of the students, defying convention, smoked a cigarette and started a fire.

Its replacement, an imposing Gothic Revival building that still stands in Lutherville, was opened the next year. Of poured concrete, brick, and hollow tile construction, the new building featured gargoyles on the turrets which flank the bronze doors of its main entrance. Today it serves as a nursing home, College Manor, for in 1952 rising costs forced the college to close.

Dr. Morris' dream of a female seminary has had its day, but the foresight with which Dr. Kurtz and Dr. Morris conceived Lutherville is attested to by its continuing prosperity. Unlike Towson, Lutherville retains the pastoral quality which prompted nineteenth century businessmen to build summer homes there. The homes are year-round residences now, Victorian, idiosyncratic, and charming in their design, and the village offers a marked contrast to the suburban communities which surround it and the high-rises that loom to the south. In 1972 Lutherville was designated a National Historic District by the United States Department of the Interior.

A turn-of-the-century winter view of the Lutherville Station shows the balcony which extended the length of the building. The station was designed by Thomas Dixon and built by John Graff Cockey in 1853.

The Northern Central was instrumental in the growth of Lutherville, for it provided fast commuter service into Baltimore for businessmen summering in the village and for students from the Maryland College for Women, originally the Lutherville Female Seminary. One student of the college recalls riding the trains into Baltimore with a beau. After a night on the town, the couple would board the last train for Lutherville for the night. At the station the campus watchman would meet them and escort the young lady back to her dormitory.

Photograph by Gwynn Crowther
Courtesy of Mabel Crowther

Completed in 1854, the first Lutheran Church was the physical as well as spiritual heart of Lutherville.

Photograph by Emma K. Woods
Courtesy of Lydia E. Berry

St. Paul's Evangelical Lutheran Church, built on the site of the first Lutheran Church in 1898, shown here in a photograph made between 1907 and 1915. The exterior of the church is marked by Gothic gables, shingle construction, and stained glass windows. A pipe organ chamber flanks the altar.

Photograph by Emma K. Woods
Courtesy of Lydia E. Berry

"Zip! Zap! Zoo!/Zip! Zap! Zoo!/Lutherville!
Lutherville! '92": the original Lutherville
Female Seminary.

Photograph by Emma K. Woods
Courtesy of Lydia E. Berry

College Manor in 1975.

Photograph by Carl Behm III

The well at the Seminary.

Photograph by Carl Behm III

Oak Grove was built as Dr. Morris' residence in
1852, and it remained in the minister's family
for over a century. The home was built of stone
sheathed in narrow, flush, vertical siding.
Elongated window casements, French doors,
and scalloped open trim are distinctive features
of the Morris home, which adjoined the property
of the Female Seminary.

Photograph by Emma K. Woods
Courtesy of Lydia E. Berry

Built between 1890 and 1895, the Von Riesen house has a classical flavor with its Greek Revival pediment. Once home of the president of the College for Women, it also housed the library.

Photograph by Emma K. Woods
Courtesy of Lydia E. Berry

Did Abraham Lincoln visit Lutherville? Francis Corkran, who built Eldon in 1855, worked in Washington and knew Lincoln. It is conjectured that the President visited Corkran at his home. Eldon's Ionic porch columns and bracketed cornices suggest the Greek Revival style. It was leveled in 1965; apartments have replaced it.

Photograph by Emma K. Woods
Courtesy of Lydia E. Berry

The estate house of Creighton, built in 1832, was part of the property purchased by Dr. Morris and Dr. Kurtz. Thus the Italianate villa with its cupola and two-story porch has the distinction of being the oldest home in Lutherville. Still in use, the house was extensively remodeled in 1944, so that today it is a two-story Georgian home.

Photograph by Emma K. Woods
Courtesy of Lydia E. Berry

In 1855 *Godey's Magazine and Lady's Book* featured plans for an octagon house, a design then in vogue. Those plans were the basis for Lutherville's own octagon house, built in 1856 for the Reverend William Heilig. On each of the three floors of the house, the octagon was divided into four square rooms and four triangular rooms. In 1947 the mansard-roofed third floor was removed.

Photograph by Emma K. Woods
Courtesy of Lydia E. Berry

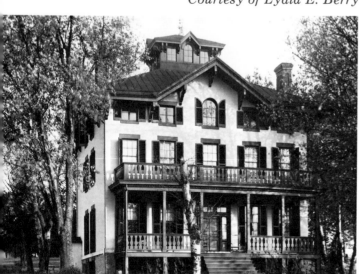

J. Frederick C. Talbott (1843-1918) was first elected to the House of Representatives in 1878. In 1864, when Harry Gilmor's raiders swept across Baltimore County, the adventurous young Talbott joined them. After serving in the Confederate Second Maryland Cavalry, he began the practice of law in Towson in 1866. Before his election to Congress, Talbott had been a delegate to the Third Judicial Convention in 1867, District Attorney for Baltimore County in 1871, and delegate to the National Democratic Convention in 1876.

*From Scharf's **History of Baltimore City and County***

From the collection of Erick F. Davis

The gardener's house at Keyburn.

*Photograph by Emma K. Woods
Courtesy of Lydia E. Berry*

Keyburn, Talbott's residence in Lutherville, stood on Front Avenue until it was pulled down in the 1920s. The Italianate villa was built by John G. Cockey in 1855.

*Photograph by Gwynn Crowther
Courtesy of Mabel Crowther*

The Woods-Littleton house, a Downing-Vaux
villa built in 1876, was the outstanding example
of Victorian architecture in Lutherville. It was
torn down in the 1960s.

Photograph by Emma K. Woods
Courtesy of Lydia E. Berry

Built in 1876, this cottage was one of a number
of the Downing-Vaux design popular in
Lutherville. The photograph was taken around
the turn of the century.

Photograph courtesy of William N. S. Pugh

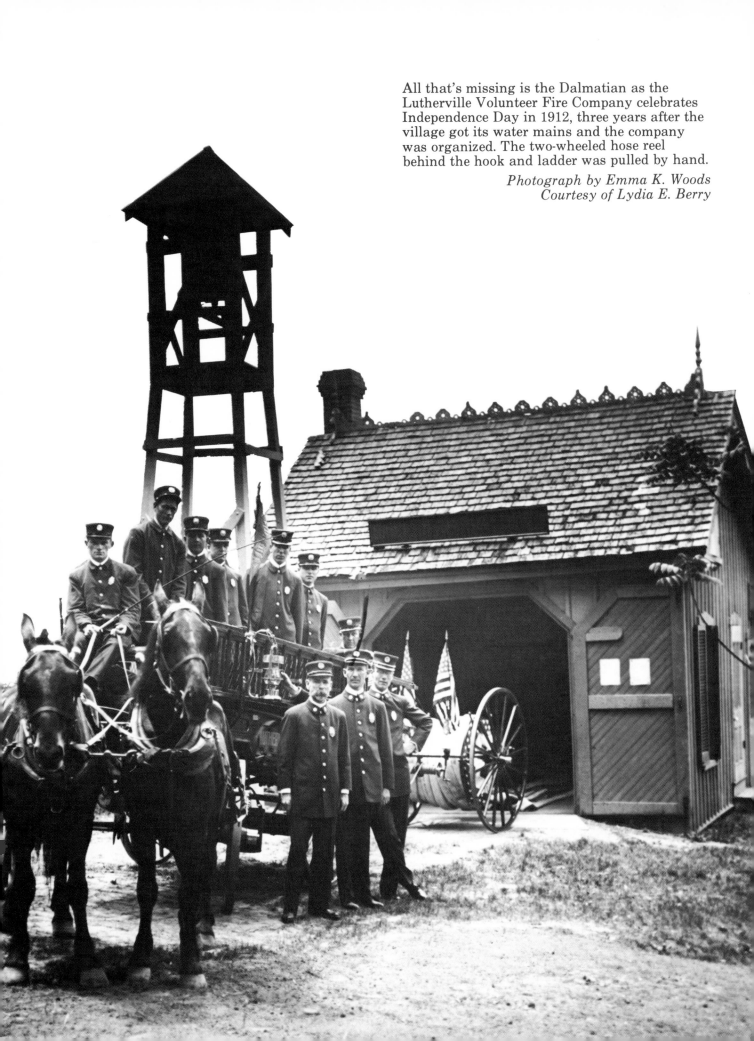

All that's missing is the Dalmatian as the Lutherville Volunteer Fire Company celebrates Independence Day in 1912, three years after the village got its water mains and the company was organized. The two-wheeled hose reel behind the hook and ladder was pulled by hand.

Photograph by Emma K. Woods
Courtesy of Lydia E. Berry

Lutherville Elementary School on Morris Avenue. The little building had two classrooms and an auditorium, but no indoor plumbing. In its day it featured a water bucket and ladle for thirsty students and a "six-holer" outdoor privy. The building was converted to apartments in 1965.

Photograph by Emma K. Woods
Courtesy of Lydia E. Berry

St. Paul's Lutheran Church was not alone in Lutherville's Kingdom of God. Three other congregations formed: Edgewood United Methodist Church, 1870; the Episcopal Chapel of the Holy Comforter, 1888; and St. John's Methodist Church, 1912, pictured here.

Photograph by Emma K. Woods
Courtesy of Lydia E. Berry

Towson's Oldest Church Building

Immediately before the War Between the States, Trinity Protestant Episcopal Church grew from the congregation of Epsom Chapel. Built in 1860, two years after the church was formed, Trinity is Towson's oldest church building. Designed by architect N. G. Starkweather, the church was built of limestone donated by John Ridgely of Hampton on a lot given by Enos Smedley. Trinity's spire was added in 1870. Thus the south facade of the church has looked the same for more than one hundred years.

Between 1891 and 1960 the building was enlarged into a cruciform by adding two transepts and lengthening the nave to form the upper part of the cross. Over the years its grounds were complemented by the addition of a Sunday School, now the Parish House (1875), the Rectory (1883), and the Memorial Hall and Education Building (1949).

Photograph by Carl Behm III

III. The Drums Of War

The War Between the States raged for four bloody years. Towson, however, was spared the devastation of a Chambersburg or Richmond, and the war actually involved the town on only two occasions. In the first weeks of the war the Towson Guards and the Baltimore County Horse Guards, pro-Union and pro-States' Rights militia units formed in the tense months prior to the outbreak of war, patrolled Towson roads and watched each other's actions. During this time railroad bridges were burned to prevent the passage of Union troops through Baltimore.

Three years later in 1864 the "battle" of Towson was fought as Major Harry Gilmor's Confederate cavalry swept across Baltimore County and routed Union troops in a charge down the York Turnpike.

Millwrights at Hoffman's paper mills in Baltimore County, Nelson Bailey (left) and James Grove enlisted in the Federal army in 1861. They were photographed when they were stationed in the South, probably in 1863. Bailey was killed on June 3, 1864, while on picket duty at Cold Harbor, Virginia. A gypsy fortune teller had predicted his death only a few days before.

The men served in Company D of the Eighty-Seventh Pennsylvania Volunteers. The Eighty-Seventh Pennsylvania was head-quartered at Cockeysville to protect the Northern Central Railroad. During the war, the soldiers marched into Towson and gave a band concert of patriotic music at the Court House.

Photograph courtesy of Joan Moore

Days of Alert: April 19 to April 29, 1861

On the evening of April 19, 1861, small knots of Towsonians gathered excitedly on the porch of Postmaster Cooper's home, at Mr. Ady's Towson Hotel (originally the Towson Tavern), and in the Smedley House. Many of the men were looking at newspapers from Baltimore City, for there was only one topic of conversation that night—the riot in Baltimore.

That morning the Sixth Massachusetts Regiment had passed through Baltimore City, part of a force of seventy-five thousand men called to Washington by President Lincoln in the wake of the secession of the states of the deep South and the siege of Fort Sumter. The men of the Sixth Massachusetts had expected trouble. They talked nervously about the taunting and shoving of Pennsylvania soldiers by rebel sympathizers in Baltimore two days before. Tension increased when each soldier was issued six rounds of ammunition as the train lumbered into the city. Ultimately, the tension, the ammunition, and a waiting mob lined up like tumblers in a lock to produce a situation from which there would be no escape. When the riot had ended, sixteen soldiers and civilians lay dead on Pratt Street.

Civil war had come to central Maryland, and accounts of the riot elicited varied responses in Towson. At Ady's Hotel, which was frequented by Southern sympathizers like Charles Ridgely, Harry Gilmor, Richard Grason, and proprietor Edward Ady, the conversation emphasized the right of the states to maintain their own sovereignty. No Northern soldiers, they declared, should pass through Maryland to wage war against a state in the South. The majority of the villagers were Union men, but the deaths of a number of innocent bystanders in Baltimore City underscored the precarious-ness of central Maryland's location. As they met on street corners or stood at the bar in their favorite taverns, they worried that Maryland—and Towson—might become a battlefield on which North and South clashed.

Sitting in his printing office on the York Turnpike, John H. Longnecker was especially concerned by the day's events. His newspaper, the *Baltimore County American,* had been an advocate of the Union in its editorials. Now, as he looked from his window across and up the Turnpike to Ady's Hotel, Longnecker wondered what the young firebrand Harry Gilmor and his brother Howard might be planning. There had been violence in Baltimore; there might well be violence in Towson. Some members of the Horse Guards, who spent most of their time at Ady's, had threatened him, and Longnecker would not put it past them to destroy his press and the little other property he owned.

Two members of the Baltimore County Horse Guards. The atmosphere of alarm that gripped Maryland following John Brown's raid in Harper's Ferry led to the formation of a number of militia units, two of them in Towson. The older of the groups, the Towson Guards, organized in the fall of 1859. On June 29, 1860, the Guards were attached to the Forty-Sixth Infantry Regiment of the Maryland Militia and issued arms. The unit numbered about fifty men, who elected Charles R. Chew of Epsom their captain. It drilled weekly in Towsontown.

The second group, the Baltimore County Horse Guards, was organized in January 1861 under the leadership of Captain Charles Ridgely of Hampton. The fifty-three-man unit was armed and attached to the First Regiment of Cavalry of the Maryland Militia on February 23. Each week the Horse Guards studied cavalry tactics at the Odd Fellows' Hall and drilled on horseback in an open area adjacent to the Court House.

Significantly, these two units differed in their loyalty. The Towson Guards were Union men, the Horse Guards, States' Rights advocates. During the week of August 19, 1861, both units were deputized by sheriff Francis Wheeler, who called upon them to "preserve the peace and order."

Photograph courtesy of Erick F. Davis

On the twentieth of April the Horse Guards made no attempt to disguise their secessionist sympathies. Most of the men wore a Maryland States' Rights badge, a silk ribbon bearing the Maryland seal crowned by Confederate flags.

From the collection of Erick F. Davis

Charles A. Conner, photographed when he was a lieutenant in the Union army, had been a member of the Towson Guards. Serving in the Seventh Maryland Infantry, he was seriously wounded.

Photograph courtesy of Erick F. Davis

The next morning the state of alert continued in Towson. The Baltimore County Horse Guards were preparing to march down the York Turnpike to Baltimore. Armed with Whitney "navy" revolvers and Ames cavalry sabres and dressed in blue frock coats, gray pants, and black slouch hats, they intended to assist the city should further violence erupt. Before they left Towson, however, the *American* came out with a broadside extra. John Longnecker had decided on a course of action. Either from opportunism or a momentary allegiance to the principles of States' Rights, he had written an editorial bound to please Southern sympathizers. As he commented four years later, "I was considered as not a loyal man on the twentieth of April." As the Horse Guards left Ady's Hotel they paused in front of the *American* office. Young Henry Shealey, standing nearby, watched as Harry Gilmor and T. Sturgis Davis led the Horse Guards in giving three cheers for Mr. Longnecker. Longnecker's editorial had served its purpose. Acting out of fear, as he later admitted, he had won the favor of those members of the Horse Guards who had earlier threatened him. Hurrahs rang out in front of the *American* office.

The Horse Guards also demanded that the Union flag flying over the Odd Fellows' Hall be lowered. Only after Longnecker and some others reluctantly lowered the colors did the Horse Guard turn and trot down the Turnpike towards Baltimore City. In the days that followed, flags were to provide the focal point for the tension which had gripped Towson.

In Baltimore the Horse Guards discovered that many officials were determined to prevent the passage of Northern soldiers through the city. That afternoon Governor Hicks had gone so far as to declare that although he loved the Union he would "suffer my right arm to be torn from my body before I will raise it to strike a sister state." This feeling, plus the need to avert further violence in Baltimore City, led Governor Hicks and Mayor Brown to order the burning of the railroad bridges north of Baltimore.

Members of the Horse Guards helped to carry out that order. As they set fire to the Northern Central Railroad bridges at Melvale, Relay House, and Cockeysville, they knew that they were helping the secessionist cause as well as reducing the chances of more violence in Baltimore City.

On Sunday morning the rest of the Horse Guards returned to Towson after passing an uneventful night patrolling the area near Fort McHenry. Captain Ridgely established the Horse Guard headquarters at Ady's Hotel, a more congenial meeting place than the hall in the Odd Fellows' building which they had shared with the Towson Guards. One of Ridgely's first orders was to send for James Sheridan, a blacksmith in the village. When Sheridan arrived, Ridgely asked him to see to it that all the company's horses were freshly shod. While he was at the hotel, Sheridan noticed that the Horse Guards were sharpening their swords on the whetstone behind the hotel.

Throughout that Sunday afternoon Ridgely was frequently in consultation with Richard Grason, one of his lieutenants. Word had come that a contingent of several thousand Northern soldiers was encamped near Hayfields, the Cockeysville farm of John Merryman, a member of the Horse Guards. They had ridden the Northern Central Railroad south as far as the burned out bridge at Cockeysville. Ridgely ordered seven of his men to Hayfields to establish an advance post from which he could be apprised of the movements of the Federal troops.

The Union men in Towson were glad to hear that Northern soldiers were within several miles of Towson. Feeling that the greatest danger had passed, Longnecker rehoisted the Union flag on the pole at the Odd Fellows' Hall. But he acted too soon. After galloping to Cockeysville to speak to the Union officers, Longnecker returned to Towson about two in the afternoon. The York Turnpike was clogged with Rebel sympathizers, "the worst crowd there that I had ever seen." Three to four hundred secessionists, "the off-scourings of Baltimore," as Longnecker termed them, had come out from the city. Their attention was now riveted on the flag Longnecker had hoisted only a few hours earlier. Cries of "Tear it down!" rang out. Henry Kone, the keeper of the Court House, heard one jeering voice ask "what that damned rag was up there for." Finally Longnecker and Richard Grason agreed that the flag should come down to prevent violence and to protect it from the crowd.

Sunday night found the Horse Guards and Towson Guards patrolling the roads—and watching each other. As Towson Guard member George Pilson, the warden of the Towson jail, put it, "We watched them and they watched us." Not surprisingly, Ridgely ordered his men to picket the roads between the Union troops at Cockeysville and Towsontown. In the minds of most of the townspeople there was no question that the Horse Guards were in arms against the troops of the United States Army. During the night Ridgely's company arrested several Union soldiers who had either deserted or gotten separated from their units. The soldiers spent

Baltimore County American
EXTRA.
TOWSONTOWN, MD.
SATURDAY EVENING, APRIL 20, 1861.

☞ Civil War is in our midst! A riot has occurred between soldiers from the North and the citizens of Baltimore, and unarmed men have fallen beneath the musket shots of soldiers from another State. We have stood long by the UNION FLAG—we have contended thus far beneath its folds, but now we must coincide with Governor Hicks and Mayor Brown, as well as with the sentiments of the people of the entire State in saying that Northern troops shall not pass unharmed through the State of Maryland, for the purpose of subjugating the South. Northern troops are now, it is said, marching to Washington, intending to *force* themselves through Maryland, and we can but say to our people, respond to the call issued by the Governor, and defend your State.

It is said that Government troops who came as far as the Gunpowder, on the Philadelphia Rail-Road, were prevented from proceeding by the bridge being destroyed, and that they are now marching on foot towards Baltimore.

The Baltimore County Horse Guards, of this place, has been ordered out, and manfully are they responding. They are now gathering, and will march before the going down of the sun.

The "Towson Guards" have not yet received orders, but are momentarily expecting them.

All is excitement here, and, with a few exceptions, all appear to be of one mind.

On the N. C. R. R., the bridges over Western Run and Beaver dams, near Cockeysville, and several bridges near the city, including the iron bridge at the Relay House, have been destroyed, to prevent the transportation of government troops from the North.

The broadside extra of John Longnecker's *American*, April 20, 1861.

From the collection of Erick F. Davis

the night in the Towson jail, and Richard Grason demanded as a condition for their release a promise that they would have no more to do with the army from which they had come—that is, with the United States Army. This demand is an indication of where Grason's loyalty, and the loyalty of the rest of the Horse Guards, lay.

The Towson Guards meanwhile patrolled the streets of Towsontown itself and also established pickets on the York Turnpike. Having experienced one mob from Baltimore, Towsonians were not eager to face another. On Sunday night a crowd of Rebel sympathizers—fortified, no doubt, by stops at the taverns on the Turnpike—marched north toward Towsontown with the intention of attacking the Union encampment at Cockeysville. It would have been no contest, of course, and in the more sober light of morning many men must have given thanks that the Towson Guards had succeeded in turning the crowd back before they clashed with several thousand regular troops.

Monday brought the news that President Lincoln had ordered the Federal troops at Cockeysville to withdraw to Pennsylvania. He did so in hopes of relieving the tension in Baltimore. At Ady's Hotel, Captain Ridgely received this order from General George H. Steuart, the commander of Baltimore City's militia: "You will follow the retreating Pennsylvania troops and report to me whether any detachments of them have been left at any point on the Railroad within the limits of Maryland. You will destroy all the bridges at intervals of one or two miles between Cockeysville and the state line." Ridgely dispatched eight men under the command of Lieutenant John Merryman to carry out the order. As the troop train cleared each bridge from Cockeysville to Parkton, the Horse Guards put the torch to it.

During the next week the Horse Guards hung the Maryland State flag over Ady's—the Rebel flag as the villagers called it—and one of the Gilmor brothers attempted to hoist a state flag on the Odd Fellows' pole, which was still bare. Several of the young Union men kept him from doing so. Then on Wednesday morning a palmetto flag was discovered flying from the Court House dome. At night the Towson Guards continued to patrol the streets to keep order;

Towson was a "border" community, just as Maryland was a border state, and the war divided some families. Archibald Harrison Davis, pictured, joined the Union army; his cousins, T. Sturgis Davis and James Davis, served the South.

On the twenty-ninth of April, Tip Yellott delivered a pro-Union speech before the ladies of Towsontown rehoisted the American flag. His uncle, George Yellott, interrupted the talk and insulted him. Later at Ady's Hotel there was "a fight, a rough and tumble fight," among the Yellotts.

Photograph courtesy of Erick F. Davis

Joshua Parlett, the blacksmith, was told to picket with five men at the six-mile stone on the York Turnpike and "to let no suspicious person pass at all." The Towson Guards also practiced with their pistols, and on Thursday their captain, Charles Chew of Epsom, accidently shot himself in the foot and resigned his command.

Finally, on Monday, April 29, the national flag was raised once again over the Odd Fellows' Hall. This time the women of the village performed the ceremony, and later in the war a Union poet would applaud "the fair of Towsontown." After some speeches, Susan Hunt and several other ladies took hold of the rope and began to raise the flag while C. N. Whittle sang the "Star-Spangled Banner." But the halyard fouled after the flag had risen only ten or twelve feet. When the handful of Horse Guards who had been watching the ceremony from Ady's porch saw that the flag had stuck, they groaned, hissed, and then gave a cheer for Jeff Davis. Finally the halyard was freed, and the national flag once more flew over Towsontown. The days of alert had ended.

OUR UNION
NOW AND FOREVER.

Union Men of Baltimore Co.
TO THE RESCUE!
RALLY!. RALLY! RALLY!
REMEMBER COL. KENLY!

Pay, Rations, Bounty Land, Extra Pay, and $100 Bounty when discharged.

HAVING received authority from Col. Wm. Louis Schley to raise a company for the Sixth Regiment Maryland Volunteers, which regiment has been accepted by the Secretary of War, we are prepared to receive recruits at CALVERTON VILLAGE, Franklin Road, about half a mile from the city limits, Baltimore county. Recruits will be uniformed and draw pay from date of enlistment. The pay is the same as of the regular United States army. Sergeants $17 per month, privates $13 per month, with good board and medical attendance. The well known military character of Col. Wm. Louis Schley, under whose immediate superintendence this regiment is to be raised, is a sufficient guarantee that the welfare of his men will receive his constant care and attention.

MARTIN SUTER, Captain,
THOS. A. MILLS, 1st Lieut.
JASPER M. SLACK, 2d do.

For information as to the character of the officers, &c., apply to John H. Longnecker, at the American Office, Towsontown.
June 6—tf.

This Union recruitment notice appeared in the American.

From the collection of Erick F. Davis

After April 29, and especially following the arrival of a large Federal force in Baltimore, Towsonians showed their loyalty by wearing silk Union badges.

From the collection of Erick F. Davis

Days of Fighting: July 10 to July 12, 1864

After the tense period from April 19 to April 29, 1861, Towson did not experience similar excitement until 1864. Many members of the Horse Guards slipped south and joined units of the Confederate army; a number of Towson Guards enlisted in the Union army. Meantime, General Benjamin "Beast" Butler occupied Baltimore City with a large Federal force in mid-May. The occupation removed any lingering possibility that Maryland might join the Southern states in seceding from the Union, and it forced the Confederate army to move through Maryland well to the west of Towson. The bloodshed that Towsonians had feared in the first weeks of the war occurred in places like Antietam, not in central Maryland. As much excitement as Towson could muster was an episode during the Gettysburg campaign, when a pass was required to enter or leave the town. Shortly after the battle Longnecker had arrested a Confederate major who was on his way to visit his family in Prince Georges County.

In 1864, however, Confederate General Jubal Early's victory at the Battle of Monocacy occupied the Union forces at Baltimore and enabled General Bradley T. Johnson to invade Baltimore County, commandeering livestock and supplies. For a short time 135 of his Confederate cavalrymen occupied Towson. Their leader was Harry Gilmor of Glen Ellen, who had risen from a corporal in the Horse Guards to a major in the Confederate cavalry.

Gilmor proved to be one of the colorful aristocrat soldiers who fostered the comparison between Confederate officers and chivalric knights. His elan and his horsemanship are apparent in this escapade recounted in *Four Years in the Saddle,* his autobiography of the war years: "We charged through two fields, across a lane fenced on each side, up to the base of the heights, and, thanks to my being the best mounted, I was the first man that jumped into the redoubt, the rest of the column close behind. When we started I was near the rear of the column; but there was no horse there that could beat my sorrel; and, as I passed along, Tom Gatch, of Baltimore County, who was doing his best, sung out, 'Hurrah for old Baltimore County!' This naturally inspired me, and perhaps made me more reckless, and may have thus been the means of saving my life; for I believe that, but for the speed with which I rode at the logs, I certainly should have been shot."

In addition to his reckless courage, Gilmor's marksmanship and devotion to young ladies added to the romantic aura which surrounded him. He regularly won bets with his pistol by plinking every telegraph pole as he galloped up a road, and once he shot a cup off Tom Gatch's head. Then, too, there are almost as many "ruby lips" as military encounters in *Four Years in the Saddle.* Gilmor described Shepherdstown as a place "famed for its pretty women," and he quickly pledged himself to their defense. In Winchester, even as the enemy was entering the town, Gilmor found time for leisurely *au revoirs.* With a friend he dismounted at the home of several young ladies to eat some cake while one of the girls served as a lookout. Women also provided Gilmor with abundant recompense for

Leslie's Illustrated Newspaper, a national publication, gave extensive coverage to the war in Maryland in 1864. Bone-weary and poorly clothed, Confederate soldiers commandeered livestock and supplies, but Gilmor claims that his men "never took a plow-horse the whole time I was in Maryland, and only such as were necessary for my purposes."

From the collection of Erick F. Davis

Gilmor capturing a train and burning the bridge over the Gunpowder, from ***Leslie's Illustrated Newspaper.***

From the collection of Erick F. Davis

a serious wound he received late in the war: "Being wounded," he wrote, "I got many a kiss from pretty girls, and without much pressing; they did not fight hard, for fear of hurting my wound!"

On July 10, 1864 Gilmor arrived in Cockeysville, took possession of the village, and burned the Northern Central Railroad bridge over the Gunpowder. When General Johnson's forces arrived, the Confederate cavalry burned the remainder of the Northern Central bridges and destroyed the railroad buildings at Texas. Johnson's army then left to rejoin General Early, pausing only to burn the summer home of Governor Bradford on Charles Street. Gilmor was left with the dangerous mission of burning the Philadelphia, Wilmington & Baltimore Railroad bridge over the Gunpowder.

That afternoon, a Sunday, Gilmor left his forces in Cockeysville while he and a few officers and friends rode to Glen Ellen. Here Gilmor surprised his family on the front steps. The reunion lasted several hours before Gilmor returned to his men. One relative, whom Gilmor entrusted with the details of his mission, offered the opinion that the family would never see him alive again.

Meanwhile, Gilmor's scouts picketed the roads between Cockeysville and Baltimore City. In Lutherville they cut down a Union flag and robbed the post office of $5.60. Five scouts also rode into Towson, cautiously entering the town from the north on the new Dulany's Valley Turnpike. Three men rode in first, then two

Harry Gilmor (1838-1883). When this photograph was taken in Baltimore in December 1862, Gilmor was a captain in the Confederate army and a prisoner of war. Attempting to "run the block" and return to Glen Ellen for a visit with his family, he was captured in Pikesville. After being held at Fort McHenry for almost three months, Gilmor was trusted to deliver himself to Major Turner in Washington. With typical bravado he took advantage of this interval between prisons to have a photograph taken of himself in uniform. He also drew a five-dollar fine for driving a carriage immoderately on Cathedral Street.

Unfortunately for the Union army, Gilmor was exchanged as an ordinary prisoner of war in February 1863. He went on to become a raider both feared and hated in the North, where he was described as a notorious guerrilla and robber. In the fall of 1864 Gilmor was seriously wounded; several months later he was captured. By the time of his capture he had risen to the rank of Lieutenant-Colonel.

After the war Gilmor returned to Glen Ellen. From 1874 to 1879 he was police commissioner of Baltimore City.

Photograph courtesy of Erick F. Davis

The War Between the States did have serious consequences for Richard Grason, pictured, who was elected to the office of Judge of the Eighth Judicial Circuit Court in 1864. Although he did not serve during the war, Grason had been a member of the Horse Guards and a proponent of States' Rights. During the week following the Baltimore riot of 1861, he was reported to have said that "if the State of Maryland did not go out of the Union, he would; if Maryland did not secede, he would."

His opponent, James Ridgely, contested Grason's election on the grounds that as a member of the Horse Guards Grason had been "in armed hostility to the United States." He also claimed that Grason "disloyally held communication with the enemies of the United States" when Gilmor's raiders visited Towson in 1864.

The Maryland Committee on Elections agreed with Ridgely. In 1865 they ruled the election a nullity on the grounds that Grason was "constitutionally disqualified" from holding the office of Judge of the Circuit Court. The testimony from the contested election provides a rich source of information on Towson during the war years.

Photograph courtesy of Frances Steuart Green

others. The villagers were startled to see them and even more surprised at their ragged appearance. One was wearing a Union uniform, another gray pants and a black velvet jacket. All obviously needed sleep. A small crowd began to gather, and a Miss Lemmon inquired about her brother, who, she learned, was in Cockeysville with the rest of Gilmor's men. As they stood in front of Ady's Hotel one of the scouts declared that he needed a hat, and threatened to break into Mrs. Mary Shealey's store to get one. E. F. Church, the editor of the *Advocate*, heard him warn that if Mrs. Shealey "has any friends here they had better get the keys." After her son William had unlocked the door, Gilmor's scout selected a slouch hat and paid for it. The scouts also entered the shop of James Pennington and took a saddle which was there for repairs. Before leaving Towson they stopped at Richard Grason's house on the Joppa Road, where the cook offered them each a glass of milk.

Late in the afternoon Gilmor and his men began their march toward the Philadelphia, Wilmington & Baltimore Railroad bridge at Magnolia in Harford County. Because his men were exhausted, Gilmor stopped at a farm and let them sleep until daylight. Early the next morning, Monday, July 11, the raiders set out again, but after crossing Bel Air Road and Harford Road Gilmor heard a shot. He galloped ahead with four men and found his ordnance sergeant, Fields, lying in front of the farmhouse of Ishmael Day near Kingsville. Fields was riddled with buckshot. There was little blood, but his face and chest were covered with dark bluish-purple spots where the pellets had entered. Though he was dying, Fields was lucid enough to explain to Gilmor what had happened. He had ridden up to Ishmael Day's house and ordered the farmer to lower the large

John Merryman was arrested and confined at Fort McHenry as a result of his activities while a member of the Horse Guards. Chief Justice Roger Brooke Taney issued a writ of *habeas corpus* in his behalf. At the order of President Lincoln, General Cadwallader refused to release his prisoner. Taney then delivered the landmark opinion *Ex parte Merryman,* in which he found the President in contempt of the Supreme Court.

*From Scharf's **History of Baltimore City and County***

Union flag flying in the front yard. When Day refused, Fields dismounted and began to tear the flag down himself. It was then that Day shot him.

Gilmor's men were enraged. They combed the nearby woods for Day, but failing to find him, they destroyed his belongings, set fire to his house, and even killed the twenty-eight-year-old family horse. Among many Marylanders, however, and especially among those who had lost property to the plundering Confederate raiders, Ishmael Day became a popular hero. Songs and poems praised his courage:

> Now let each heart, in our cause take a part,
> Do his duty—watch, fight and pray,
> Shoulder his gun, stand by, never run,
> And imitate Ishmael Day.

After sending the dying Fields to Wright's Hotel on the Harford Road, Gilmor pressed on. The next morning he captured and burned two trains at Magnolia. He took General Franklin of the Union army prisoner and destroyed the bridge over the Gunpowder. Considering that he had a force of only 135 men, his success was remarkable.

Gilmor left Magnolia about four o'clock and headed west. Despite warnings of Federal soldiers in the area, he decided to enter Towsontown. He galloped into the village, pistol drawn, with a handful of his men. All was quiet. He drank a glass of ale at Ady's and talked to some old friends while the rest of his men came into the town and assembled in the square in front of the hotel. The Rebels chopped down the flagpole there and cut the Union flag into pieces. It was now the early evening of July 12, and the stage was set for the "battle" of Towsontown.

Union cavalry in Baltimore had heard that Gilmor was near Towson. About sixty men, probably including the Towson volunteers organized by L. M. Haverstick after the Battle of Monocacy, rode north on the York Turnpike. Although Gilmor believed a much larger force was approaching, he insisted on having "at least a brush" with the enemy. He was, after all, playing before a home crowd. Gilmor ordered fifteen of his men to charge the advance guard of the Union cavalry and force them back into the main body of their unit. They were then to fall back, encouraging the Union cavalry to pursue them at a gallop. Meanwhile, Gilmor waited in Towsontown with the rest of his men, who were exhausted and anxious about the impending battle. "I expect the band will go up tonight," one man said, but Gilmor noted that no one suggested they retreat without a fight. They waited, sabres drawn, for his order to charge.

The sound of hooves and pistol shots grew louder. The small advance unit was very near. Then he ordered his attack. His men filled the air with a roar of Rebel yells and charged down the York Turnpike. The sudden counterattack bewildered the Union troopers. They whirled about before Gilmor's men could reach them and began a race back to Baltimore City. Some of Gilmor's men kept up the pursuit as far as Govanstown.

After the skirmish Gilmor left Towson, passed to the west of Baltimore, and rejoined General Early's army. The town had had a good scare, for many Towsonians believed that the Confederate raiders might destroy their homes or the Court House in retaliation for Union destruction in Virginia. But in the end Gilmor's cavalry left Towson unharmed, and at the end of the Civil War the town was little changed from the way it had been in 1860.

William H. Ruby, a bugler for the Horse Guards, participated in the burning of the Northern Central bridges. Although he did not serve in the Confederate army, he remained a staunch advocate of the Southern cause. When Southern fortunes were at their lowest in 1865, he founded a pro-Confederate newspaper in Towson, the *Maryland Journal.*

*From Scharf's **History of Baltimore City and County***

IV. Ashes To Aspirations

If one main event after the Civil War was a disastrous fire, other events were constructive. A railroad began, a bank was founded, two churches were consecrated, a hospital arrived, and a school system grew in Towson.

Looking south at the 500 block of York Road shortly before the great fire of 1878. The road was little changed from the dirt turnpike down which Harry Gilmor led his cavalry charge against Union troops. These were the days of carriages, hitching posts, and boxes to protect young trees from gnawing horses.

Directly behind the tallest trees stands the original Odd Fellows' Hall. The Towson Lodge was chartered on January 10, 1852, and later that year the Odd Fellows moved into this hall on the York Road, built at a cost of four thousand dollars. The row of buildings stood opposite the present location of the Towson Theater.

Photograph courtesy of
M. Eliza Bosley and Marie Bosley Kade

On January 26, 1878, the row of buildings in the 500 block of York Road burned. Only the outer walls of the Odd Fellows' Hall remained standing. The fire had begun in Shealey's store and spread rapidly when fifty pounds of powder exploded.

Because Towson had no fire company, the thirty-three member Towsontown Militia under Captain David Gregg McIntosh was called out. The unit, composed of Confederate and Union veterans, had been organized in August 1877 and later won a reputation for excellent drill and discipline.

The Odd Fellows estimated their loss alone at ten thousand dollars. Only their books and regalia were saved.

Photograph courtesy of Erick F. Davis

The Odd Fellows' building before the fire.
Photograph courtesy of the Odd Fellows

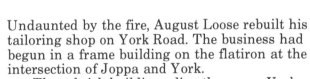

Undaunted by the fire, August Loose rebuilt his tailoring shop on York Road. The business had begun in a frame building on the flatiron at the intersection of Joppa and York.

These brick buildings directly across York Road from the present Towson Theater were probably photographed in the late teens. York Road was still unpaved, but sidewalks and cut-stone curbing had been added.

Photograph courtesy of
M. Eliza Bosley and Marie Bosley Kade

An 1877 map of Towson. The properties destroyed by fire the next year may be seen on the west side of the York Road between Pennsylvania and Allegheny Avenues.

The terminus of the horse-drawn Baltimore & Yorktown Turnpike Railway Company stood a short distance to the south of the Odd Fellows' lodge. The trolley's single track is marked by the line running up the center of the York Road.

The Baltimore, Philadelphia & New York Railroad is a cartographer's dream, and a rather ambitious one at that. Not until 1881 was any track laid on the line that was to become the Ma & Pa.

From Hopkins' **Atlas of Baltimore County**

The Ephrium B. Almony house on York Road breathes the quiet style of life in Towson a century ago. Standing as early as 1877, the house was wrecked in 1948 for Carter's Furniture Store.

If such houses are victims of twentieth-century commerce, their porches are casualties of twentieth-century lifestyle. Once an architectural staple, the porch became vestigial when radio, television, air-conditioning, air pollution, and crime drew people indoors. Gone with the porch is the small town camaraderie of strollers stopping to chat and sip lemonade.

Photograph courtesy of Frank C. McCrystle

A Record of Towson Life
A Century Ago

Newspapers came to Towson with the Court House and the schools. Such weeklies as *The Jacksonian* (1850), the *Maryland Standard* (1859), and the *Possum Hollow Gazette* (1859) furnished conversational fodder for Towson homes, bars, and barber shops.

The most important of Towson's early newspapers were the *Baltimore County American* (1850), later the *Union*, the *Baltimore County Advocate* (1850), and the *Maryland Journal* (1865). During and after the Civil War these weeklies channeled heated opinion on local and national issues.

Less ambitious, the *Baltimore County Herald,* though Democratic in its politics, enjoyed a life of provincial news and reflection. There were partisan editorials and angry letters to the editor, of course, but the paper's chief interest since its founding in 1869 was town-talk. Read today, the four-page weekly is an index to the life of a sleepy Victorian Towson.

There was sports coverage. From an 1870 issue, for example, a Towsonian could learn that the local Caseys had lost a cliffhanger to the Govanstown nine, 42 to 34. Or he might plan his weekend around the 1876 announcement of a pigeon shoot in Govanstown.

The "financial" editor was continually grousing about the high cost of eating in 1882, when Towson turkeys cost eighteen cents a pound, eggs forty cents a dozen, and beer nine dollars a barrel. Christmas holidays along York Road that year no doubt featured fewer white meat sandwiches, stronger egg nog, and weaker ale.

Personal news was always apparent in the *Herald.* Readers in 1882 learned that Colonel Harry Gilmor was recuperating from the painful effects of an extracted tooth, that Judge Richard Grason and family had just returned from a vacation in Ocean City, that Dr. J. W. Hawkins had been thrown from his buggy, and that Miss Mollie Ady had just opened "a ladies' and gents' store" specializing in underwear.

The police beat had its space. In 1876 readers were no doubt shocked to learn that "our County was on a rampage last Tuesday, no less than six pugilistic encounters occurring between here and Waverley." A crime wave was probably apace in 1882 when the *Herald* warned Towsonians: "Look out for burglaries. Keep your gun well loaded." Later in the year they were gratified to learn that "Judge Phelps...has sentenced a wife-beater to be whipped with seven lashes." The local mystery of 1882 was how a fine Alderney cow had got down a

twenty-five foot dry well from which she was pulled to safety.

Holding its rural readership in mind, the paper kept agricultural items prominent. Weather predictions and "how-to" articles on plowing, fencing, preserving fruit, using manure, analyzing soils, and fattening geese were common.

Health was a main concern as well. Besides reporting local illnesses, the paper included advertisements such as "Ladies' Tonic: The Great Female Remedy" for "any weakness or complaint common to the sex." This remarkable potion sold for only a dollar a bottle. No wonder that physicians had to advertise on the front pages.

Other advertisements abounded. Towson businesses from George Schmitt's tin store to A. H. Krout's brickworks to J. H. Myers' ice cream saloon puffed their products in the 1870 *Herald.*

Another standard front-page feature was literary. Readers gloried in short stories such as "A Cross Husband; Or, How He Was Cured," and pondered poems like "Into Each Life Some Rain Must Fall." An 1882 reader could chuckle at pastoral riddles such as, "How to get cowslips in winter? Drive your cattle on ice."

Throughout, the *Herald* kept a chatty tone. The editor complained frequently of being distracted in his offices by squealing pigs and the nuisance of cattle and horses being driven down the York Road. Echoing the perennial complaint of a local citizen, he was moved to reflect in 1876 that "reform is practically dead in this county." The editor's localism was perhaps his link with his readers; it made him "human," "one of us." What editor today could write as did the *Herald* editor on December 2, 1882, that "a turkey would be very acceptable to the local editor during the holidays"? And what modern journalist could have reported in the next issue that his wish had been granted?

It is the humanness of the *Herald* that makes the paper lively reading today. And for a one dollar yearly subscription, Towsonians had fifty-two weeks of overwhelmingly "good" news.

East Towson:
An Afro-American Refuge

While the first black people may have arrived with the Towson family in 1752, we do know that in 1798 Ezekiel Towson held two slaves, William four, and Francis six. Many of the large land-owning families, like the Chews, Cockeys, Ridgelys, and Stansburys, kept slaves, but during the first half of the nineteenth century the number of free blacks in Baltimore County was increasing. By the terms of Charles Carnan Ridgely's will, for example, all of his three hundred slaves under the age of forty-five were freed upon his death in 1829.

By 1860 the number of free blacks in the county exceeded the number of slaves. The best indication of the number of black families in the Towson area is the election record of 1870, which shows that thirty-seven black men living within a one-mile radius of the Court House had registered to vote. These free blacks owned or rented houses and plots along the York Turnpike near present-day Stoneleigh, along Regester Avenue, near the the Court House, in east Towson, and in Sandy Bottom (once the site of a Ridgely slave quarters just north of Towson). Indeed, one old-time resident of east Towson has said that there was less segregation in housing in Towson prior to World War II, for blacks lived throughout the area.

East Towson is a black community that has endured. Probably the first black landowner there was Daniel Harris, who bought one-and-a-quarter acres from the Payne family in 1853 for $187.50. After the Civil War the community grew. The opening of the street railroad in 1863 made it easy for blacks to get to jobs. And the jobs were available. Many blacks were farm workers, especially at Hampton, and sons accompanied their fathers to the fields during peak seasons until at about age twelve they began to work full time themselves. In addition, blacks worked as cooks and porters in Towson businesses, as construction workers and teamsters, and as maids, butlers, and later chauffeurs.

Photograph by Coke Hagepanos

Built on Jefferson Avenue in 1881, twenty years after its congregation formed, the Saint James African Union Methodist Church remains an important force in the religious and cultural life of East Towson.

Its second story—the church sanctuary— was added in 1904.

Photograph by Carl Behm III

Undoubtedly, east Towson has endured because most of its residents have been homeowners. Of some five hundred blacks living in east Towson during the 1890s, seventy-five percent owned their homes. This high rate of ownership may be due largely to the Relief Association of Baltimore County. Founded in 1882 for the "purpose of buying, selling, leasing, mortgaging, improving, and otherwise disposing of land" to relieve the sick and needy, the Association held some twenty-five to thirty acres in east Towson, land which it sold mainly to blacks.

Even from small wages—in 1910 a farm laborer at Hampton earned six dollars per week—families saved enough to buy land and to build homes. Most built their own houses. From such sacrifice and hard work grew the belief that one's home should be respected and, most importantly, retained at any cost. For the home was a refuge, socially and economically, from the white world all around. Parents passed on this ethic to their children.

Home ownership fostered stability and stability fostered a strong sense of community, a spirit of sharing and cooperation. For example, one resident recalls that during the Great Depression there were no soup lines in east Towson: "We took care of our own." And if a man coming home from his job passed a neighbor building a barn or patching a roof, he would invariably take off his coat, hang it on the fence, and work along until dark.

Often black ownership was threatened, and old-timers bitterly remember real estate speculators who duped those who could not read or write. In 1964 the spectre of urban renewal threatened the community, but the twin ethic of ownership and neighborly cooperation prevailed. Today, however, the community is threatened from within. Many young blacks leave east Towson with little desire to return, an exodus that began during World War II. With them goes the hope of the community continuing into another generation.

Dedication of the newly remounted bell at St. James Church, November 1975. When weakened timbers forced the removal of the bell from the roof of the church, the parishoners determined to re-erect it. The bell is not only important to the congregation of St. James; it once rang over a church in Govans. And prior to 1893, when the horse-drawn streetcar had its terminal near Urban's Saloon on the York Road, the bell hung at the car barn. It was used to announce the departure of the streetcar for Baltimore City.

Photograph by John W. McGrain

Mt. Moriah Lodge of the Masons was built on the northeast corner of Washington and Chesapeake Avenues. The hall, constructed at a cost of seven thousand dollars, was dedicated on June 9, 1880. The two-story building of pressed brick provided the first permanent house for the Lodge which had been established in 1865.

*From Wilson's **Towson: Then-Now***

Alex Parlett at the window of his home at York and Joppa Roads where in the last quarter of the nineteenth century he kept his blacksmith shop. A gasoline station now stands in its place.

Towsonian Elmer Parks has said that this once was the sheriff's house and that a whipping post stood in its yard.

Photograph by Charles W. E. Treadwell Courtesy of Hilda N. Wilson

Towson's "Famous" Railroad

Rarely do seventy-seven miles of railroad win a place in the hearts of people the equal of the affection Towsonians felt for the Maryland & Pennsylvania Railroad, the "Ma & Pa." But then the Ma & Pa was not just another railroad. To the end, it remained scenic rather than efficient, quaint rather than business-like. George Hilton, the author of a book-length history of the railroad, crystallized the spirit with which most Towsonians viewed the Ma & Pa: It seemed, he wrote, like a "model railroad at the scale of 12 inches to the foot."

The Ma & Pa meandered through Baltimore, Harford, and southern York counties, curling around the hills and bridging the valleys. The track contained 476 curves and few significant straightaways. One hundred and eleven trestles and bridges punctuated the right-of-way, an average of one every seven-tenths of a mile. Small wonder, then, that the Ma & Pa highballed at twenty miles per hour and that a Sunday driver in the last years of the railroad's life could make the trip from Towson to York in one-third the time it would have taken him by train.

The early history of the Ma & Pa is a chronicle of ambitious plans, false starts, and telling poor decisions. From the 1830s Baltimore City businessmen contemplated building a railroad to Philadelphia via Bel Air. In the 1860s the Maryland Central Railroad Company was chartered and granted a right-of-way, but no construction began. In 1873 another company, named the Maryland & Pennsylvania Railroad but not *the* Ma & Pa, got so far as to grade a right-of-way from the Northern Central line at Relay House through Towson and a

A narrow-gauge railroad reached Towson in 1882. Here, a Baltimore & Lehigh Railroad train stops at the Towson station in 1899.

Engine Number 7, a 4-4-0 with forty-nine inch drivers, was built in 1887. When the railroad converted to standard gauge in 1900, this narrow-gauge engine was sold. It remained in service in Ohio until 1928.

Photograph courtesy of Charles T. Mahan

Scenery was one thing the Ma & Pa had in abundance. In this 1942 photograph, a southbound train leaves the Sheppard Station for Baltimore.

Photograph by Charles T. Mahan

short distance beyond, but the company went bankrupt before any track was laid. In 1877 Harford County businessmen dreamed of a railroad which would enable them to transport milk and other products into Baltimore. These businessmen made two decisions which were to determine the character of—and the ultimate demise in Maryland of—the railroad which became the Ma & Pa. First, they decided to build a narrow-gauge railroad because they wanted to have the ability to interchange with the Peach Bottom line, which had just been built from York to Delta. Second, they decided upon a very difficult route which would provide local service to Laurel Brook, Fallston, Vale, Bel Air, Forest Hill, and other Harford County towns.

This group acquired a right-of-way into Baltimore through a merger with a proposed suburban line, the Baltimore, Hampden & Towsontown Railway. They named their company the Baltimore & Delta Railway and began laying track in 1881. On April 17, 1882, service between Baltimore and Towson was inaugurated. Passenger trains made eight round trips daily.

In August 1882, the railroad merged with the Maryland Central, for its directors were still thinking in terms of completing a right-of-way to Philadelphia. There was hardly the capital available to justify such a plan, however, and the Maryland Central Railroad very shortly fell into bankruptcy. A new Maryland Central Railway Company was formed in 1888, and the next year the company acquired control of the York & Peach Bottom Railroad.

On May 19, 1889, through service between Baltimore and York began. The event marked an actual as well as a symbolic change in direction. The dreams of a right-of-way to Philadelphia receded, and the railroad recognized its destiny. In 1891 the Maryland Central and the York & Peach Bottom merged to form the Baltimore & Lehigh Railroad Company. The birth throes of the Ma & Pa had not ended, however. The Baltimore & Lehigh Railroad went under in the depression of 1893, and the northern and southern portions again became separate. This separation widened when the new Pennsylvania company, the York Southern, converted to standard gauge in 1895. The revived Maryland section of the railroad, which retained the Baltimore & Lehigh name, did not have the capital necessary for conversion until 1900. The next year, under the leadership of the Alexander Brown Company, the Baltimore & Lehigh merged with the York Southern. When this merger was approved in February 1901, the Maryland & Pennsylvania Railroad was finally born.

The Ma & Pa prospered for the next fourteen years. Thereafter, an ever-expanding and improving network of roads made trucks and cars expedient alternatives to the railroad.

In the 1950s, after decades of eking out an existence, the Ma & Pa began to run consistently in the red. Through freight service between Baltimore and York was curtailed; passenger service was reduced to one train daily in 1951 and discontinued in 1954. The Maryland trackage, which provided the company with a minimum of freight revenue and a maximum of maintenance expense, carried its last train in June 1958.

In its last years the popularity of the Ma & Pa among railroad buffs led the company to add the phrase "The Famous Ma & Pa" to the logo on the company's rolling stock. Yet the picturesque quality of a railroad which twisted like a blacksnake through the rolling countryside foretold its eventual demise. Curves and bridges bring tears of joy to the railroad hobbyist, but tears of another kind to a railroad accountant. A right-of-way designed for a narrow-gauge railroad serving many small county towns made the Ma & Pa popular—and slow and expensive to operate. Now all that remain are the memories and pictures of Towson's "famous" railroad.

While Towson was a principal source of passengers for the Ma & Pa, it offered little freight. There were two sidings at Towson, as well as a siding into the power plant at Towson State University. In this photograph, taken in March 1942, a covered hopper car unloads bulk cement for the Clark Concrete Company, which was located at the end of Washington Avenue.

In the first days of the railroad's operation, mischievous Towson youths played with the cars left on the sidings. The *Baltimore County Union* of August 5, 1882, condemned the sport: "The practice of boys getting on coaches belonging to the Narrow Gauge, placed on sidings, and enjoying a ride thereon, may result in serious accidents. On Thursday last two boys adopted this practice, and run [sic] one of the cars off, and subjected the workmen to much trouble in replacing the same."

Photograph by Charles T. Mahan

Engine Number 43 at the Towson Station, October 4, 1941.

The Station Master's car is parked on the north side of the station.

Photograph by Charles T. Mahan

Dismantling the bridge over the York Road.

Photograph by John W. McGrain

Leaving the Towson Station, Engine Number 6 crosses the York Road bridge just north of Susquehanna Avenue. When this picture was taken in 1952, this 4-4-0 with sixty-two inch drivers was at the end of a long career. Built in 1901 for the newly created Maryland & Pennsylvania Railroad, Engine Number 6 was sold for scrap shortly after this picture was taken.

Stebbins-Anderson's buildings are visible under the bridge.

Photograph by John W. McGrain

85

Two views of the Joppa Road trestle, which is now the intersection of Joppa Road and Goucher Boulevard. The earlier photograph was taken before Towson Estates was constructed in 1929. The development shows up clearly in the later photograph, taken in November 1942, in which the station may be seen just beyond the trestle.

Photograph by Charles W. E. Treadwell
Courtesy of Hilda N. Wilson

Photograph by Charles T. Mahan

The end of an era. On June 11, 1958, the last train to run on the southern end of the Ma & Pa crosses the Washouse Trestle just before passing the Oakleigh Station.

Other signs of change are also evident. In the foreground, a ramp for the new Baltimore Beltway is under construction. From the 1920s it was evident that competition from trucks and automobiles doomed the Ma & Pa. Chatterleigh now occupies this land.

Taking up track at Towson Heights early in the summer of 1958.

Photograph by Charles T. Mahan

Photograph by Charles T. Mahan

The Immaculate

In 1884 the forerunner of the present Church of the Immaculate Conception and its parochial school complex was built on Ware Avenue to meet the needs of Towson's Catholics. The establishment of a Catholic church was spurred by the arrival of many Irish workers on the Baltimore & Delta Railroad, whose tracks reached Towson in 1882. Originally, the church was named for St. Francis of Assisi.

Here the class of 1906 poses in front of the frame building which served as both church and school. The stairs led to the church on the second floor. The doors beneath them opened into a three-room elementary school. Consistent with American Catholic custom, a school was erected before a separate church building was begun.

With the class is Reverend Philip H. Sheridan, Pastor.

Photograph courtesy of Madeline E. Weis

Mass was first celebrated in the present stone church of the Immaculate Conception in 1904. A new elementary school was constructed in 1922; Towson Catholic High School opened in 1928.

Photograph by Carl Behm III

Towson's First Bank

Towson's first bank helped establish the commercial importance of the county seat. D. G. McIntosh and some business associates founded the Towson National Bank in 1886 and kept its offices in McIntosh's "little red brick building" at Washington and Pennsylvania Avenues. By November 13, 1886, the *Baltimore County Union* could comment, "Towsontown's National Bank is now in full operation and already the town has taken on a more important air. Our people may not be so progressive as some, but vulgarly speaking, we get there all the same."

In 1912 the Towson National Bank moved to Court House Square, and in 1959 it merged with the Mercantile Safe-Deposit and Trust Company.

Instrumental in founding the Towson National Bank was David Gregg McIntosh (1836-1916). A South Carolinian, McIntosh had read law before the Civil War, during which he rose to the rank of colonel. McIntosh saw action from the first shot fired at Charleston harbor to Appomattox. In one engagement he had two horses shot from under him. At the war's end, refusing to surrender, he lay in the swamp of the Appomattox during the day and slipped through Grant's lines by night.

Penniless, McIntosh came to Towson in 1868 and established a law partnership with Arthur W. Machen and Richard S. Gittings. From 1879 to 1883 he was the prosecuting attorney for Baltimore County.

In this picture McIntosh sits astride his horse, Osler Joe, in front of his home on Pennsylvania and Washington Avenues, present site of the Campbell Building. His residence was diagonal to his law offices.

Photograph courtesy of J. Rieman McIntosh

The old Towson National Bank was built in 1887. After 1912 it housed the Baltimore County Bank, which was founded in that year.

Photograph courtesy of Maryland Historical Society

When the Towson National Bank moved to Court House Square, Washington Avenue was still a dirt road and a hitching post stood at the curb. Note that when this photograph was taken, the nine-foot clock, one of Towson's best known landmarks, had not yet been installed.

Photograph by Charles W. E. Treadwell Courtesy of Hilda N. Wilson

Another Inn at the Crossroads

Bosley's Hotel stood where Hutzler's is now. This picture, showing the bearded proprietor Charles Bosley at the left, was snapped in 1892.

For at least part of its history, the Bosley offered its own version of the racial doctrine of separate but equal. The hotel featured parallel bars served by a single tapmaster between them. After entering through separate doors, blacks sat at one bar, whites at the other, facing each other over mugs of lager beer.

Photograph courtesy of
M. Eliza Bosley and Marie Bosley Kade

How many would recognize this to be York Road in 1894? This starkly dramatic picture shows the entrance to the Sheppard-Pratt Hospital. Though the house still stands, dirt roads and the trolley tracks which lined the east side of the turnpike have long since disappeared.

One sign of modern times is the sidewalk, which appears here more than fifteen years before the first pavement was laid in central Towson. It ran to Sheppard-Pratt and is a measure of the importance of the trolley in the era before the automobile.

*Photograph courtesy of
Sheppard-Pratt Hospital*

From Cell to Sunlight: The Sheppard-Pratt Hospital

Conditions in insane asylums and public almshouses were grim before 1850. In nineteenth-century America insanity was tantamount to crime and was treated as such. Most counties then kept alms and work houses where paupers, disorderly persons, vagrants, and the insane were indiscriminately lodged. As late as 1842 Charles Dickens complained about outrageous conditions in a New York asylum. And Moses Sheppard was horrified at the treatment of insane paupers in Baltimore. Visits to insane asylums, as well as mental disturbance among some friends, prompted Sheppard to earmark a fortune to aid the insane.

The site he chose for a haven was a 340-acre farm, Mt. Airy, six miles from Baltimore on the York Turnpike. Construction began in 1860, three years after Sheppard's death. In the spirit of his will, all was done for the comfort of the patient. Fresh air, greenery, recreation, and commodious rooms and board revolutionized the care of the mentally disturbed. One need only glance at the pictures to see the predominance of flowers. In large measure they are emblematic of a new concept in mental asylums. In parlors and hallways as well as in meadows and gardens, their presence is a continual reminder of the founder's concern for the patients, an innovation that took psychiatric care out of the dark ward into the sunlight.

In 1896 when Enoch Pratt bequeathed over one million dollars to the institution with the proviso that its name be changed to "The Sheppard and Enoch Pratt Hospital," he signalled a shift in direction that was more than semantic. The asylum, or place of retreat and custody, became a hospital, a place of treatment and cure. Sheppard-Pratt began to attract leaders of medicine and psychiatry and to become a nucleus for psychiatric care.

In spite of later financial problems, the Great Depression, the hardships of two world wars, and personnel and patient shortages, the hospital has continued the founder's and the benefactor's mission. Yet it never lost its personal, individual concern for the patient. Examples abound, but two—in the jaws of the Depression—are representative. In 1932 a Cadillac was bought to take patients on excursions and picnics to the northern countryside. And in 1935 a shopper was hired for people who could not leave the hospital; her semi-weekly returns from local stores brought delight to many patients. Today, through in- and out-patient treatment, Sheppard-Pratt has expanded its community health programs and special services for alcoholism and drug addiction. Its international distinction for patient care, medical advances, and humanitarian effort has been well earned by its treatment of more than twenty-one thousand patients from its origin until 1975.

Sheppard-Pratt Hospital in 1892. The main buildings rise like a Victorian Camelot from the original 340 acres of Towson countryside. Workers cut foundation and stairway stone from a quarry opened on the grounds, which also yielded an excellent quality of brick clay. When a manufacturer was contracted to produce bricks for six dollars a thousand in 1860, rapid construction seemed imminent. But the Civil War and the terms of Sheppard's will delayed progress. Railway service was appropriated for soldiers and supplies, and blasting powder could not be had for the quarry.

Moreover, Moses Sheppard's directive that only the interest on his bequest be used delayed the project longer. Indeed, construction proceeded so slowly that a proverb developed among Baltimoreans and Towsonians reluctant to finish a job: "When the Sheppard is finished, I'll do it." Not until 1880 would the brickwork be completed.

Calvert Vaux, the New York architect who had recently laid out Central Park, designed the main buildings. They have been designated United States Historic Landmarks.

Photograph courtesy of Sheppard-Pratt Hospital

The founder, Moses Sheppard (1775-1857). A virtually indigent Quaker lad of eighteen, Sheppard started work as an errand boy in Baltimore in 1793 and soon amassed wealth as a provisions merchant in the thriving port. A true citizen, he served as director of several city businesses and banks, exhibited interest in the new railroads, and served as Warden of the Poor and member of the Inspection Committee of the City Jail. A true Friend, his philanthropy was manifold: educating Quakers, aiding the tribes of New York as a member of the Indian Affairs Committee, and resettling free Negroes in Liberia as a manager of the Maryland Colonization Society. But his most lasting humanitarian act was the bequest of his estate (less two thousand dollars for friends and servants) of $571,440.41 to found Sheppard Asylum for the "moral treatment" of the mentally ill.

Photograph courtesy of
Sheppard-Pratt Hospital

The benefactor, Enoch Pratt (1808-1896). Coming to Baltimore from his native Massachusetts in 1831, Enoch Pratt acquired his fortune as a hardware merchant. Associated with Moses Sheppard in the American Colonization Society and the Baltimore Library Company, the Unitarian businessman became interested in the Sheppard Asylum. Having already established a library in Baltimore with his gift of a building and over one million dollars, Pratt in his will made the Trustees of the asylum his residuary legatee for what finally amounted to $1,069,400.41. His only stiuplation was that the title of the institution be changed to "The Sheppard and Enoch Pratt Hospital." He also desired that it take in "the indigent insane in the most advisable manner, at very low charges or absolutely free...."

Photograph courtesy of
Sheppard-Pratt Hospital

The Gatehouse (1860), known to Towsonians as the "Hansel and Gretel House," was the first of Sheppard-Pratt's buildings to be completed.

Photograph courtesy of
Sheppard-Pratt Hospital

The Casino's summer-house style echoes the concern for patient recreation. Built in 1901, it houses facilities for art work, billiards, bowling, music, cards, and dramatic productions. The Casino also serves as a center for occupational therapy. During World War II patients made garments, surgical dressings, and traction splints for the Red Cross, Children's Aid Society, and British Relief. The baseball game in the foreground evinces the therapeutic value of exercise, fresh air, and interpersonal relationships so crucial to Sheppard-Pratt's philosophy. As an early medical director said, "There is little in the Hospital that is stagnant or depressing, and there is comparatively little opportunity for brooding, self-pity, and fantasy....Every patient who is accessible is given the opportunity to do something."

Photograph courtesy of
Sheppard-Pratt Hospital

The Sheppard-Pratt drug room early in the century. Its very presence signals the shift from asylum to hospital. Later, in 1930, when a certified pharmacist was appointed, a new era in medical care began. Hydrotherapy, or the use of wet sheet packs to calm patients, gave way to chemotherapy, which often helped cure neurotic patients.

Photograph courtesy of
Sheppard-Pratt Hospital

A patient's parlor. Note the decorative touches, especially the ever-present plants.

Photograph courtesy of
Sheppard-Pratt Hospital

A Vienna at Towson:
Furthering the Hospital's Mission

If humane concern for the patient is the heart of Sheppard-Pratt's mission, pre-eminence in medical and psychiatric thought is its brain. It was the second Medical Director at the hospital who averred that a core of scholars must be at every hospital worthy of the name. Over the years at least four scholars at the hospital have earned national reputations as rare blends of scholar-teacher-physician.

At Sheppard-Pratt from 1922 to 1930 was Dr. Harry Stack Sullivan. Though trained as a Freudian, in time Sullivan became the leading exponent of the dynamic-cultural school of psychoanalysis.

Dr. William Rush Dunton is known as the Father of Occupational Therapy. Coming to Sheppard-Pratt in 1895 and serving there for twenty-nine years, he recognized that occupational therapy, or creative and productive activity, is a crucial adjunct to treating the mentally ill. The many recreational opportunities at Sheppard-Pratt breathe Dunton's spirit.

Dr. Lawrence S. Kubie came to the hospital in 1959 as Director of Training with many scholarly honors derived from his gifted lectures and nearly three hundred scholarly writings on the behavioral, medical, and social sciences.

Formerly President of the American Psychiatric Association, Dr. Robert W. Gibson,

pictured, is also Sheppard-Pratt's fourth Medical Director. During his tenure since 1963, he has blended the hospital's in-patient care with an extensive out-patient program incorporating many educational and mental health services.

Photograph by M. E. Warren
Courtesy of Sheppard-Pratt Hospital

The families of some patients built residences on the hospital grounds. In this picture is the Norris Cottage at the Osler Drive entrance. Osler Drive was opened in 1964. At first it was to be called "St. Joseph Road," after the Catholic hospital to be built nearby. But when a church organization objected, it was renamed "F. Scott Fitzgerald Drive" for the novelist who had lived at La Paix. Then Sheppard-Pratt suggested that the road be designated to commemorate Sir William Osler, first physician-in-chief at Johns Hopkins. County Executive Agnew agreed, and the road became "Osler Drive."

Flags, ferns, and Japanese lanterns bedeck Norris Cottage on a Fourth of July early in the century. Busy Victorian decorative arts were still very much in style.

Photograph courtesy of
Sheppard-Pratt Hospital

A main improvement in school furniture was the Soper desk, invented in Baltimore in 1864. Its movable seat allowed an aisle between desks. These desks are part of the Knights of Columbus float on the Fourth of July, 1964.

Photograph by John W. McGrain

Grammar, Hickory, and Character

American education, says Donald Barr, has moved from the blackboard to the bulletin board. The bulletin board is a museum, a static place where students pickle their past—what they wrote, drew, calculated. The blackboard, conversely, is a dynamic studio where students experience the present—writing, drawing, calculating. In the first half of our schools' history the blackboard was central and its relationship to the curriculum direct.

That curriculum allowed few electives. According to the 1864 report of Libertus Van Bokkelen, Maryland's Superintendent of Education, "In every district school there shall be taught Orthography, Reading, Writing, English Grammar, Geography, Arithmetic, the History of the United States and good behavior."

At least in part students learned these subjects at the blackboard, in full view of others in the class. The teacher would demonstrate, the pupils imitate. Maps were drawn, words spelled, dates recorded, handwriting tested, words defined, arithmetic problems solved, and sentences parsed and diagramed. Grammar was always important. Minnie Lee Davis recalled that she was required to parse, or to analyze grammatically, Milton's *Paradise Lost* while still in the grades. After a turn at the board there was glory or embarrassment, guidance or chastisement. Education was public, and everyone witnessed success or failure.

A first-grade reader of 1883. Parents then paid seventy-five cents for their children's use of books, for only in 1896 did Annapolis authorize the state to purchase them.

Education in the county has always been progressive. In 1915 the *Baltimore County Course of Study* was published and soon became a national text. By 1921 three hundred elementary school systems in forty states used it.

Courtesy of Baltimore County Board of Education

Discipline was keen. Schoolmasters did occasionally use the hickory stick until it went out of fashion by 1911. One principal sent the boys into the nearby woods to gather switches that he would later use on them. Whipping offenses included smoking and chewing tobacco, habitual among older boys. Some boys even carried pistols to class, a practice that occasioned whippings as well as a shocked notice in the *Baltimore County Union* of 1885.

Often students were disciplined as much for backwardness and ignorance as for disobedience. Their punishments included long written tasks, problem solving, and detention after school. Still another was making miscreant boys sit with the girls.

Both curriculum and discipline, however, were means. The end was character. In the best tradition of Thomas Arnold's Rugby School the aim was to build ethical citizens. In a letter to the *Democrat & Journal* in 1911, Lida Lee Tall, Baltimore County's Supervisor of Grammar Grades, wrote, "It is only by associating with the best writers of the world's literature that ideals are set up with children." In the same issue, Arthur C. Commer, principal of Towson High School, wrote that "by precept, by example, and by every illustration...the student is taught that the highest attainment is character." When he added that "Honor has been enthroned; the rod destroyed; the child elevated," modern education began in Towson.

Public education in Maryland began in 1848 when Baltimore County created the first school system in the state. In January 1849 sixty schools opened. Among them was Towson's first schoolhouse, a one-room log cabin on the east side of Delaware Avenue a short distance south of Joppa Road. It is now a residence, though much changed from the days when a large open fireplace warmed schoolchildren sitting erectly on long wooden benches.

Since this modest beginning, daily attendance in Baltimore County schools has increased one hundredfold from its first year average of 1,858 pupils. In Towson a new school was soon warranted, and at a cost of slightly more than seven hundred dollars a lot was purchased on the west side of Virginia Avenue south of Shealey, and a frame schoolhouse was erected. At the new school the instructors were men, who received an annual salary of 250 dollars for teaching a curriculum limited to the primary grades. In 1873 another school, a two-story brick building on East Chesapeake Avenue, was built for eight thousand dollars. In the same year the curriculum at the Towson school was extended so that it roughly paralleled that of a junior high school today. Just after the turn of the century, when three more years were added to the curriculum, Towson's first high school was born.

After fire destroyed the East Chesapeake Avenue school in 1906, a new building was constructed on Allegheny Avenue at Central while classes were held in various places in Towson. The new school opened in 1907. It is the building with a white cupola on the left side of this panorama. To the north is the present Towson Elementary School; it was built in 1925 as a junior-senior high school.

Photograph by Carl Behm III

The history of Towson High School points up the recent proliferation of Baltimore County schools, for gone are the days when students from Cockeysville and Hyde traveled south to attend class in Towson.

When Towson High School began, students in all eleven grades went to the same building. In 1925 high school and junior high school students moved from the building on Allegheny Avenue to a new school just to the north on Central Avenue; the Allegheny Avenue building was afterwards used for the elementary grades. Then in 1948 Towson Senior High School, pictured here, opened at its present location on Cedar Avenue. For the first time senior high, junior high, and elementary school pupils each reported to a separate building. From one school had grown two, and from two had grown three.

Photograph by Carl Behm III

Carver Colored High School on Jefferson Avenue was organized in 1939.

Schooling for blacks was established in Maryland in 1864. These schools were supported solely by taxes collected among blacks. In 1872 Baltimore County provided for a black school in Towsontown on the condition that a furnished house be offered free of rent. Indeed, it was not until 1897 that Baltimore County appropriated any money for black school construction, $283.39 for a building in Towson.

Before 1939 there were no black high schools in Baltimore County. Eligible students wanting to continue their education beyond the seventh grade had no choice but to enroll in a black high school in Baltimore City.

Photograph by Carl Behm III

V. Into A New Century

A pastoral intersection north of Towson at the turn of the century. Where a shopping center now sprawls, automobile horns blow, and exhaust fumes rise, rolling farmlands once graced the eye of a stroller looking east from York Road along Seminary Avenue.

Photograph by Gwynn Crowther
Courtesy of Mabel Crowther

The York Turnpike

At the turn of the century, the York Road was still owned by the Baltimore and Yorktown Turnpike Company. Chartered by the General Assembly in 1804 or 1805, this private company maintained toll booths and kept the road in repair for over a century.

The need for an improved system of roads had been recognized as early as 1787. Passage from farm to port had made the York Road crucial, so in that year the county began plans for a turnpike. It had not completed the road, however, before the Turnpike Act expired and the private company took over the project.

Two years after the State Roads Commission was established in 1908, Maryland reacquired the Baltimore and Yorktown Turnpike Road. Toll booths were pulled down, turnpikes were pulled up, and travelers rode free once again.

Richard Parker, Gate Keeper, stands at his tollbooth on the York Turnpike near Linden Avenue shortly after the turn of the century.

A tollgate-keeper's life was not always uneventful. Frederick T. Rinehart, sixty-five year old employee of the Dulaney's Valley Turnpike Company, was brutally murdered in 1906. Highly publicized trials followed the crime. Ultimately, his murderer was sentenced to be hanged and the killer's accomplice to be imprisoned for eighteen years.

Photograph courtesy of Robert T. Parker

The original turnpike consisted of a sixty-six foot right-of-way on which a forty foot strip was cleared of stumps and rocks. In 1894 the York Road between Towson and Baltimore was widened to one hundred feet.

This 1899 photograph shows the tollbooth on the west side of the York Turnpike opposite Linden Terrace. The toll bar serves as a reminder of the root of the word "turnpike," which derives from the sharp pikes which blocked a private road and were turned aside only after a traveler had paid his toll.

The building on the left side of the picture, originally the Bowen home, was already a century old when this photograph was taken. It is now the Tuxedo House.

Photograph courtesy of Hilda N. Wilson

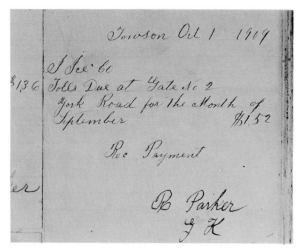

Courtesy of Raymond A. Seitz

Sales and Scales

Albert M. Weis ran a general store just north of the firehouse from 1886 to 1923. Here Weis sold groceries, hardware, feed for livestock, and the cigars he manufactured in a back room. A German who moved to Towson from Pennsylvania, Weis first opened a shop in the Shealey building, which later became the firehouse, but soon purchased this building on the York Road. Two years after establishing his business, he was able to return to Pennsylvania, marry, and bring his bride to Towson. Older Towsonians remember him rocking on the back porch of the store and reading a German newspaper.

In 1914, three years after this photograph was taken, gasoline pumps were installed. The next year the store was enlarged and outfitted with all new fixtures. Goucher College purchased Weis' property in 1921, and after leasing the store from the college for two years, Weis sold his stock to Elmer Corbin. Corbin operated the general store until the 1950s.

Photograph courtesy of Madeline E. Weis

Mr. Weis is seen here with his son Henry and daughter Madeline in 1914. A prototypal general store, Weis' sold everything from onions to buggy whips to ax handles. And, of course, penny candy. Barely visible to the right of Miss Weis' shoulder is an electric coffee mill—the first in Towson. The case at the left contained, among other things, violin strings and jew's harps.

Long hours were the rule for the family. The store was open every day from seven a.m. to nine p.m. and until eleven on Saturday nights. Miss Weis recalls that as a girl she began work daily at seven, had breakfast, attended Immaculate School, returned home to lunch and to tend the store while her parents ate, finished the school day, and then worked in the store until seven in the evening.

Photograph courtesy of Madeline E. Weis

Towson Public Scales,	May 31 1911
Weighed for	D. F. Cathcart
A load of	Hay
	Gross 7500
	Tare 2300
Weighing 50	Net 5200
	A. M. Weis Weigher.

On the south side of his York Road store Weis maintained public scales on which he would weigh cattle and loads of hay and other produce farmers were transporting to market. Madeline Weis remembers well how her father would frequently be awakened at two or three in the morning by a well-directed pebble thrown against his bedroom window. Farmers, wishing to be at the Baltimore markets before dawn, needed him to weigh their wagons, and when he had done so, they hurried on into the night. Miss Weis also remembers cattle drives down York Road in the first decades of this century and the difficulty with which her father and the farmers would maneuver the frightened animals onto the scales.

Courtesy of Raymond A. Seitz

The Herzogs built a home between their tinner's shop and Weis' general store in 1911. This picture was taken as the family sat on the porch on July 4, 1924. At the left is the founder of the business which his son John (right) and his grandsons have continued.

Photograph courtesy of Mrs. John Herzog

Towson's tinner. Just north of Weis' store on York Road was the shop of W. Robert Herzog, who stands on the porch.

Photograph courtesy of Mrs. John Herzog

The Phipps' businesses. The Phipps story is a model of immigrant adventure. In the nineteenth century, the family came from England to find a home and establish a business. The father and one son arrived first. As the mother and two other sons were sailing to join them, the father died. Though the senior Phipps' dream went unfulfilled, he had succeeded in bringing his family to a new land, and his sons went on to establish two Towson businesses.

James (at the left) and Alfred (in the window) ran the bootery pictured here at 414 York Road, now part of the Finkelstein building. The third brother, Harry, operated a meat market at 406.

Between the stores and partially visible on the right in this photograph was the Feast house, which once served as Towson's post office.

Photograph courtesy of Mrs. Russell Hall

The Dienstbach Shop. Henry Dienstbach, pictured, carried on the harness and saddle shop established by his father. The store was located to the north of the Phipps bootery.

When this picture was taken, more and more automobiles were sputtering up and down the York Road past the harness shop. The transition from the age of horses to the age of the internal combustion engine had begun, just as inside the Dienstbach shop electric fixtures hang above a pot-bellied stove. Pot-bellied stoves and harnesses soon became items of pleasure, not of necessity.

Photograph courtesy of
Mrs. George Radebaugh, Jr.

Yoicks!

The Elkridge Club stands on the site of Governor Bradford's country home. When these pictures were taken at the turn of the century, Elkridge was a fox-hunting club.

Photograph courtesy of J. Rieman McIntosh

These riders are on the drive leading from Charles Street.

Photograph courtesy of Taylor A. Birckhead

Flivvers

Members of the Reckord, Haile, and Blakeney families pose in a Model T Touring Car parked beside the "little red brick building" in 1911.

The celebrated "Tin Lizzie," which could clip along at forty miles per hour while getting thirty miles to the gallon, featured such long-gone items as a rubber hand horn and, directly below it on the running board, a carbide generator to make acetylene gas for the headlights. The headlights as well as the kerosene running lights below the windshield were lit with a match.

Note that the license plate is slanted off to the side to allow free swinging of the hand crank. Miss Margaret E. Haile recalls some of the idiosyncracies of the "Tin Lizzies": "The Ford Fracture was bad enough—that broken wrist that could be caused when an engine backfired as it was being cranked—but too often a forgetful driver would leave a car in gear. Then, when he cranked it and the engine caught, the monster would roll forward and run him down."

Photograph courtesy of Margaret E. Haile

A Towson Fourth of July in 1911. These four "Tin Lizzies," with their brass radiators, were owned by Walter P. Reckord, the first automobile dealer in Baltimore County. They are parked in front of a house on Pennsylvania Avenue at the present site of the Mercantile Bank parking lot.

Photograph courtesy of Margaret E. Haile

"I think I can!" The hill into Towson revealed the fundamental deficiency of the battery-powered trolley. When the battery was low or the load heavy, the car could not make the grade.

The unpredictable battery did endear itself to one group of passengers. When the trolley was not able to run, the news was telegraphed to the stations on the Northern Central line, where many county children learned that they would have to take the day off from school.

Photograph by Charles W. E. Treadwell
Courtesy of Hilda N. Wilson

The importance of a connection between the Northern Central Railroad station at Lutherville and the county seat at Towson was recognized quite early. This stagecoach provided a nineteenth-century solution to the problem.

Photograph courtesy of Towson Library, BCPL

Towson's "Toonerville Trolley"

For eleven years residents of Baltimore County traveling south on the Northern Central line for a day of business at the county seat or a day of learning at the high school or the State Normal School completed their journey on the Towson & Cockeysville Electric Railway.

The "Toonerville Trolley" went as far north as the Northern Central station at Timonium. Here Northern Central passengers from Glencoe or Cockeysville would board the trolley for a twenty cent ride into Towson. Along the way the trolley would pick up passengers at Ridgely Avenue, Melanchton, Bellona, and Seminary Avenues in Lutherville, and Sandy Bottom. Then it would struggle up the steep hill to Bosley Avenue—if the car were full, the men would have to get off and "help" it up the grade—and travel south to its terminal at Bosley and Chesapeake. Soon the line was extended a short distance east on Chesapeake Avenue, and a car barn was built on Washington Avenue at the present site of *The Jeffersonian* building. What made the line unique was that it was a battery-powered railway. Battery-powered streetcars had been tried in the 1880s in Baltimore, but they proved impractical. By 1912 battery technology had advanced, however, and the Towson & Cockeysville Electric Railway's first car was capable of hourly round trips between Timonium and Towson from seven in the morning until ten at night. In 1916 a new battery car was ordered from the J. G. Brill Company in Philadelphia. An eighteen foot longitudinal seat car, it covered 113 miles each day until the line was abandoned in October 1923.

The *Democrat & Journal* of August 24, 1912, reported on the maiden run: "After the sun had gone down on last Monday and the little village of Timonium had settled into eventide repose, the Towson & Cockeysville Electric Railway entered upon its life of activity....In an instant, as though by magic, people living in the houses *en route* came out and gave the visitor a warm welcome. Soon Lutherville was reached and the fair village was soon the scene of animation. Sweethearts ceased to tell tales of love, and even Judge Frank I. Duncan deserted the judicial pose and threw his hat up in the air and yelled 'Here she comes.' When the electric car whistle announced its arrival in the county seat many mistook it for an automobile."

Within a month the newspaper noted that the trolley "hauled 4,619 passengers last week."

Photograph courtesy of William N. S. Pugh

Laying track for the "Toonerville Trolley." These photographs were taken just south of Lutherville in 1911. After leaving Towson, the trolley line ran over a private right-of-way sixty-six feet wide. It passed through Lutherville on Division Avenue.

Although the company planned to extend the trolley line to Cockeysville, its inability to get permission to cross the Northern Central Railroad tracks halted construction at Timonium.

Photographs courtesy of William N. S. Pugh

The Hay Wain. This scene was photographed
on Front Avenue in Lutherville shortly after the
turn of the century. To the right is Keyburn; to
the left, barely visible, are the Northern Central
Railroad tracks.

Photograph by Emma K. Woods
Courtesy of Lydia E. Berry

VI. Milestones

Most historians date the end of the Victorian Age with the outbreak of war in Europe in August 1914. Similarly, two events in 1915 and 1917 may be said to have begun the modern era in Towson. The coming of the Maryland State Normal School and the Black & Decker Manufacturing Company brought the provincial capital to state and national notice. Although the school and the business each cited the "country" atmosphere of Towson as a reason for locating there, their arrival foretold Towson's evolution from a rural town to a burgeoning suburb.

A plat of Towson in 1915.

In the quarter century from 1890 to 1914 Towson had experienced the following new developments: the admitting of the first patient to the Sheppard-Pratt Hospital (1891), the building of the Mt. Olive Baptist Church at Baltimore and Pennsylvania Avenues (1892), the founding of the Mt. Calvary African Methodist Episcopal Church on Eudowood Lane (1900), the completion of the new church of the Immaculate Conception (1904), the opening of the Towson High School building at Allegheny and Central Avenues (1907), and the inauguration of service on the Towson & Cockeysville Electric Railway (1912).

In 1915 the first classes were held at the Towson campus of the Maryland State Normal School. The farmland between Joppa Road and the Maryland & Pennsylvania Railroad tracks owned by D. G. McIntosh became the home of Black & Decker two years later.

*From Bromley's **Atlas of Baltimore County***

Sidewalks paralleling a dirt road, a carriage passing an automobile—such sights characterized the York Road in the teens of this century.

From the left are Lee's Store on the corner of York Road and Pennsylvania Avenue; the Odd Fellows' Hall; the Firehouse, just visible under the trees; Bosley's Hotel, where Hutzler's stands now; and the Baltimore County Bank.

Photograph courtesy of
Helen Frankenfield Reckord

"Brass radiator" Fords belonging to the congregation of the First Methodist Church line York Road on a Sunday about 1914.

Towson Methodists had formed a congregation in 1869. Two years later they moved into this church at 622 York Road. The Investment Building stands in its place today.

Photograph by Charles W. E. Treadwell
Courtesy of Hilda N. Wilson

111

"And Gladly Teach." The crisp neatness of the 1904 graduates was no doubt engendered by the "Regulations" of the school. As schoolmarms, these ladies would transmit their own customs to generations of Maryland schoolchildren. Prim poses were the rule, and written on the page of a Maryland State Normal School yearbook just after the turn of the century was the comment, "One girl was almost hysterical on finding, after the picture was taken, that her feet were showing."

Photograph courtesy of Towson State University

Towson: Normal School to University

The Maryland State Normal School was founded in 1866 "for ladies exclusively." It was charged with the preparation of teachers and, at the suggestion of State Superintendent of Education Libertus Van Bokkelen, included a model school for "student teaching."

The first campus was at Red Men's Hall on Paca Street in Baltimore City, though the students stayed with private families for three to five dollars weekly. Needing better accommodations, the school moved in 1872 to a colonial mansion at Charles and Franklin Streets, later the home of the Athenaeum Club. Soon that campus became overcrowded, and after an appropriation of one hundred thousand dollars by the General Assembly, the students reported in 1876 to a new campus on Lafayette Square. The two-year course was extended another year to include Latin, chemistry, English literature, geometry, physiology, and military drill, for by then men were being admitted.

Because the rural schools then stressed grammar, spelling, and arithmetic, the preparation in these subjects at the Normal School was keen. In the history of the English Language course, for example, professor and first principal M. A. Newell drilled his students in philology and the metrics of poetry to increase their facility with the mother tongue. Between similar drills in other courses, recreation was rare, for the student was regarded as an intellectual animal. Students no doubt rejoiced at *the* social event of 1885, the Apron Soiree, to which each female came in an apron of her own making with an escort of her own (or her parents') choosing.

By 1905 the program had been extended to four years—two academic years for those who had not finished high school and two professional years for those who had.

By 1911, more than 350 new teachers were needed annually for Maryland elementary schools. But the Normal School was able to furnish only eighty teachers yearly. The old campus at Lafayette Square had become inadequate. The 1912 Report of the Building Commission of the Maryland State Normal School cited poor conditions such as fire hazards, bad ventilation and lighting, too few and too small classrooms and laboratories, noisy streets, absence of dormitories, and lack of open ground for exercise. Moreover, because the Normal School was preparing teachers chiefly for rural classrooms, the Commission thought a country campus to be desirable. And because Baltimore County employed more elementary teachers than any other Maryland county in 1911—3,819—it seemed the ideal home for a new campus.

The Commission proposed fifteen sites for the school, including three plots in Towson—the Chew property of 425 acres just north of the town, the Offutt property of forty acres on Chesapeake Avenue, and the seventy-one-acre Allen-Nelligan land just south of Towson on the York Road. One attractive feature of all the Towson plots was their proximity to the York Road streetcar line and the Maryland & Pennsylvania Railroad tracks. In those days when public transportation was more used than talked about, these assets were major.

The Commmission won a bond issue of six hundred thousand dollars, and after it spent 83,735 dollars for the Allen-Nelligan property, construction began in 1914. Sleepy Towsontown was awakened by blasting for excavation. Some Towsonians remember that people walked through town plugging their ears and grumbling about progress with every blast.

By the next year classes had begun. The campus included a classroom/administration building (later Stephens Hall), the Newell Hall dormitory and dining room, and a power plant. Already there were the Allen cottage and Glen Esk, the Nelligan house, as well as some farm buildings. The campus was an academic island amid greenery and farmlands.

Sample examination from 1875. The literacy of students during those early years of the school extended to a working reading of Anglo-Saxon, or Old English. One can assume their facility with Middle and Modern English.

Courtesy of Towson State University

Sarah E. Richmond (1843-1921). One year after graduating from Western High School, the sixteen-year-old Miss Richmond was teaching in the Number Eighteen Primary School in Baltimore City at one hundred dollars a year. During the Civil War, when Baltimore teachers were asked to swear allegiance to the United States or resign, she resigned her post because of her family's Southern sympathies. In 1866, she left to enter the first Maryland State Normal School class. On her graduation Principal Newell asked her to teach in the Normal School for the next year. Miss Richmond then started a tenure with the school that was to last fifty-five years.

In 1909 she became its fourth principal. Tirelessly pressing for a better campus, she often worked until four in the morning writing letters to influential alumni and officials for help in securing country grounds for the Normal School. Whenever the General Assembly met, the ubiquitous Miss Richmond was there in the halls, plumping for the "school question."

No one was more important than Sarah Richmond in determining the move to a new campus. After seeing the Normal School through its first years in Towson, she resigned as principal and in 1917 became Dean of Women. In 1924 Richmond Hall was named in her memory.

Photograph courtesy of Towson State University

Stephens Hall construction in 1914.

Photograph courtesy of
Towson State University

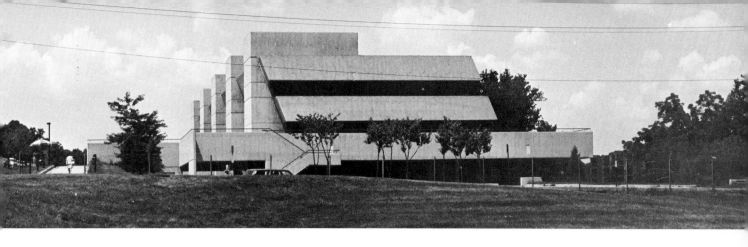

Building Styles: Cathedral to Manor to Bunker

The three administration buildings reflect variant attitudes towards education. The Victorian cathedral Gothic of the Lafayette Square Building (1876) echoes the late nineteenth-century's "religion of learning" ideal. In manorial Jacobean style Stephens Hall (1915) breathes the Deweyan philosophy of educating the "whole" student for the world. And the new—nameless—Administration Building (1972) suggests the retrenchment of modern American education in the 1970s.

"Gladly would they learn—and serve." Though the periodic table of elements was shorter, this chemistry class photographed between 1915 and 1918 still worked hard to master it. During the World War I years, Principal Henry S. West offered the school to Towson and Baltimore County groups as a community center. Students worked with neighborhood women and faculty members to sew, roll bandages, and knit scarves for the boys "over there." Many of the ladies in this class were probably Red Cross members.

*Photograph courtesy of
Towson State University*

Glen Esk, built in 1905, was the home of the Nelligan family. It became the residence of the principals and presidents of the Maryland State Normal School at Towson. Glen Esk was used by the school heads through the tenure of President Hawkins until 1969. Now it is partitioned into offices for counseling services.

Here, Miss Lida Lee Tall, sixth principal of the school, stands on the porch around 1920. During Miss Tall's tenure, from 1920 to 1938, faculty meetings were held at least once or twice monthly. All these were academic meetings, for administrative details were taken care of via the faculty mail box.

*Photograph courtesy of
Towson State University*

College as Bibliocentric Universe

Learning becomes democratized as the closed book cabinets in the Lafayette Square library in 1905 give way to the open stacks of the Stephens Hall Library of 1918. The Albert S. Cook Library, completed in 1969, is designed to shelve six hundred thousand volumes and seat six hundred readers.

Photographs courtesy of Towson State University

The Model School

A class of the Model School at the Maryland State Normal School in the mid-1920s. Three teachers or training students supervise the split activities in Stephens Hall. From 1866 the Model School provided opportunity for "student teaching."

Photograph courtesy of
Towson State University

Our Gang. This class from 1926 might well have been photographed on a back lot of MGM.

Photograph courtesy of
Towson State University

Van Bokkelen Hall was built in 1933 to house the Model School.

Looking east over the Towson campus in 1930. The campus farm (where today are Lida Lee Tall School and Smith Hall) was bounded on the south by the Ma & Pa Railroad line. The farms, meadows, and woodlands beyond York Road suggest the expanse of the area's rural environment. At an elevation of 450 feet, the campus commanded a good view of its surroundings.

Student Styles

Picture-posing tells much about the need to project an image. Either the late teens photograph of the Newell Hall sitting group or that of the improbable 1941 study group before Stephens Hall would be cogent visual aids for a "Please-send-money" letter home to Dad. The *bon vivants* in the tree are from the 1970s.

Photographs courtesy of Towson State University

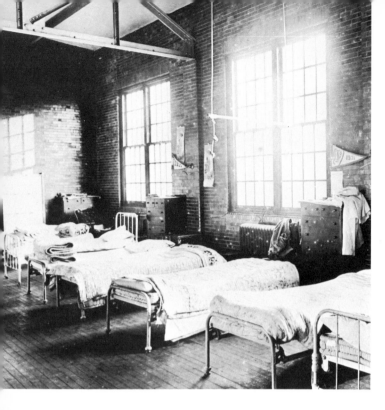

On the second floor of the power plant in the early 1920s was a men's dormitory. Its Spartan character makes one wonder about the gaiety of the Jazz Age and agree with the building's nickname, "The Barracks." Still, somebody's spirit and loyalty were keen: note the class pennant over one cot.

Photograph courtesy of Towson State University

Newell Hall Dining Room about 1928. This was the annual scene of the Old English Christmas dinner, when an orchestra played in the balcony, medieval-costumed students and faculty dined, jesters pranked, and staff caroled. The student Chimes Guild sang and played chimes five nights weekly during dinner to provide grace for the meal.

Photograph courtesy of Towson State University

In 1955 clay tennis courts and the Ma & Pa track lay where Linthicum Hall now stands. A men's dormitory, West Hall, is in the background. During the 1920s a barn and other outbuildings stood on the Ward and West Hall grounds; thus students dubbed the area "Pig Sty Hill."

Photograph courtesy of Towson State University

During World War II, the student weekly, *Towerlight*, ran such advertisements selling cigarettes and morale. The weekly was filled with items about the war; "News from Camp," about Towson students in arms, was a running feature. Practical pieces, such as "What to Do in an Air Raid" and "Buy Defense Bonds in Registrar's Office" shared the page with debate on such topics as "Are the German People at Fault?" And while students and faculty bought war bonds, practiced civil defense, and planted Victory Gardens, a 1942 columnist advised her readers, "With men so scarce, start plotting right now whom you can entice to join you on the 21st for a really hep evening. My date figures he can buy me a War Stamp corsage with the money I save him. Tricky, huh? Pass the word around."

Courtesy of Towson State University

As We Grow Larger

After World War II professional programs multiplied. A liberal arts course of study for veterans was added in 1946, the same year that a curriculum for junior high school teachers was established. A pre-school program emerged the next year. In 1958 a Master of Education course was instituted. In 1960 a course for the preparation of high school teachers began. In 1963 the school became Towson State College when it established a liberal arts foundation.

These were the years of President Earle T. Hawkins, who presided over the groundbreaking for eleven new buildings during his tenure from 1947 to 1969. In 1949 there were forty-nine faculty members and 764 students; by 1965 there were 171 professors and nearly five thousand students, including night school enrollees. President Hawkins' theme was "As we grow larger," an appropriate one that echoed the equally rapid growth of the Towson community at large.

During the administration of President James L. Fisher this growth has continued. In 1976 the faculty numbered about 450 and the full-time day student population 8,400. Seven new buildings have been started or completed since his coming in 1969. Moreover, President Fisher originated many new programs such as the second bachelor's degree, college in escrow (for high school students), a literacy crusade, and majors in nursing, medical technology, and dance. He has pledged the institution to an ongoing commitment to the liberal arts. His establishment of the Towson Foundation, a private funding program, is unique; because the state finances only forty-eight percent of the Towson operation, private fundraising is crucial. President Fisher's most publicized accomplishment was his role in gaining university status for Towson in 1976.

Dr. Earle T. Hawkins, president of the college from 1947 to 1969.

Photograph courtesy of Towson State University

The administration of Dr. James L. Fisher, current president of Towson State University, began in 1969.

Photograph courtesy of Towson State University

Bastille or Blighted Eden?

Those were electric days between 1967 and 1972. In Viet Nam the war still raged while American bombs pounded Cambodia. If politics became a fashion, morality in politics became a watchword. One heard continually of moral commitments to the war and moral commitments against it. It seemed that everyone took an inflexible stand for or against, because if politics are negotiable, a moral system is not. The merging of politics and morality paralyzed both, so that only events could determine outcomes.

The activities of April and May, 1972, encapsulated it all. Towson State College radical groups mobilized to occupy Linthicum Hall, march under candlelight to the Court House, insist that military recruiters be banned from campus, and demand that the college abandon its position of political neutrality. Campus conservative groups argued for free job choice, punishment for illegal entry of campus buildings, and college support for national policies.

President James L. Fisher tried to reconcile both sides. The College dropped all warrants against those charged with occupying Linthicum because innocent bystanders were apparently involved, allowed military recruitment to continue, and maintained its political neutrality so that its members would be free to take partisan positions.

Beneath the surface of the topical issues festered a central question: Does an institution such as Towson State owe primary allegiance to the state that supports it or to the intellectual tradition of dissent that engenders it? Never answered, the question may be raised again in other ways in other times.

Some saw the College as a Bastille; others saw it as a blighted Eden. Like Towson itself, the College was changing, and change left it divided and writhing in self-doubt.

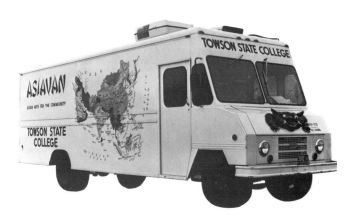

Town and Gown Affairs

At the annual Fine Arts Ball students, faculty, and members of the Towson community dance harmoniously. The Asia Van also evinces the close ties between the university and its neighbors. It enables Towson State to share its collection of Oriental art with area schools and community groups.

Photograph courtesy of Towson State University

Students lollygag before the Ball. Proceeds from the gala establish scholarships for Towson fine arts majors.

Photograph courtesy of Towson State University

127

Time, Gentlemen!

Time did indeed run out for two old Towson hostelries, the Six-Mile House, razed in 1915, and the Smedley House, destroyed by fire the next year.

The Six-Mile House on the York Road in 1914 during construction of the Maryland State Normal School. The *Union News* of June 12, 1915, reported, "The Yard at this old hostelry in the early days of travel by wagon and stage was always crowded with wagons, which made it their headquarters for the night." The large house on the east side of York Road just above the barn is the Wilton Greenway home. The view is from the site of Stephens Hall, the first administration building at the Towson campus.

*Photograph courtesy of
Towson State University*

HOTEL SMEDLEY
TOWSON, MD.

Erected the same year as the Baltimore County Court House

WILL SERVE THE HOME-
COMING BANQUET . . . . .

We are Ready to Serve the Public!

SPECIAL ATTENTION TO
AUTOMOBILE PARTIES.

Our Lawn Beautifully Illuminated at
Night by Electric Lights.

MAKE THIS HOTEL
YOUR HEADQUARTERS.

When Enos Smedley opened his hotel where the Armory now stands, he drew his guests from the Court House and from Baltimore City. County politicians gathered there to debate; city folk came to summer. In the 1880s an improved and renovated Smedley House touted itself as a "delightful, pleasant and reasonable resort." Its 1883 advertisement in the *Baltimore County Herald* boasted that it was free of mosquitoes and had the best of water. And the new narrow-gauge railroad had heightened its convenience for businessmen, who could commute to Baltimore for thirty-two cents per day.

Smedley himself was a farmer, and he continued to work his Pennsylvania land even after he opened his Towson business. Usually, he visited the hotel only about four times a year.

The alliance of the Court House and the hotel was close. The row of lawyers' offices lining Chesapeake Avenue west of the hotel was known as "Smedley's Row." Jurors and others doing business at the Court House frequently found accommodations at the Smedley House.

Photograph courtesy of Towson Library, BCPL

A 1912 advertisement.

The Smedley House burned in 1916 after serving Towson for sixty-two years. A cook was killed in the fire.

Photograph courtesy of John E. Raine, Jr.

The fire chief's car across the street from the pumper.

Photograph courtesy of John E. Raine, Jr.

Photograph by Charles W. E. Treadwell
Courtesy of Hilda N. Wilson

Loch Raven

Sunday visits to the country often included a walk across the suspension bridge at Loch Raven dam. When this picture was taken in the teens of this century, the old, or lower, dam had been in use for more than thirty years.

The Gunpowder River was first mentioned as a source for Baltimore City water as early as 1836, but it was not until 1875 that the growing pollution of Lake Roland made a new water source imperative. Indeed, the *Baltimore County Union* of July 10, 1875, offered this comment on the city's water troubles: "The Baltimore *Bulletin* says the peculiar flavor of the water the people in the city are compelled to drink is produced by men bathing in Lake Roland. It

may be proper to add that the *Bulletin* man don't [sic] always tell the truth." Regardless, many Towsonians refused to drink water when they ventured into the city.

Ground was broken in December of that year for a dam at Raven's Rock, where two months before Harry Gilmor had deposited "a number of fine bass." The dam and a tunnel to bring the water from the Gunpowder to Lake Montebello and Lake Clifton in the city were completed in 1881 at a cost of 4,500,000 dollars. Thirty million gallons began to flow through the tunnel each day to quench the thirst of a growing population.

Photograph by Charles W. E. Treadwell
Courtesy of Hilda N. Wilson

By 1912 a new dam was started after the city bought an additional 168 acres at Glen Ellen. These engineers contemplate work on the new dam, a task made easier because the seven-mile tunnel to Baltimore City completed in 1881 was adequate. This tunnel is still in use today, though the flow has been reversed and it now conveys filtered water from Lake Montebello to Towson.

The tunnel was a marvel of nineteenth-century engineering. Twelve feet in diameter, it was blasted through rock at depths from sixty-five to 360 feet below the surface.

Another example of the care expended by the predecessors of these engineers was their decision to use both sand and a mechanical system to filter the water. It contributed to the fact that no case of typhus has ever been attributed to the water from Loch Raven.

Photograph by Charles W. E. Treadwell
Courtesy of Hilda N. Wilson

Robert Gilmor gave the name "Raven's Rock" to an outcrop on the Gunpowder near his home. He had found the name in his friend Washington Irving's *Legend of Sleepy Hollow.* When the dam was constructed there, *Loch* Raven may have been chosen in deference to the Gilmors' ancestral Scotland.

Perhaps, too, the crenelated castle of the gatehouse of the new dam was inspired by Gilmor's romantic house, Glen Ellen. If so, it seems a regretful nod to the way of life of the great estates which faded slowly out of existence in the twentieth century.

Photograph by Charles W. E. Treadwell
Courtesy of Hilda N. Wilson

The scenic beauty of Loch Raven still attracts Sunday visitors. The new dam was raised another fifty-two feet in 1923, giving it a total height of 240 feet. Nearly two hundred million gallons of water now flow from the reservoir on a hot day.

Photograph by Carl Behm III

Drilling for Profits: Black & Decker

In 1910 two young men, S. Duncan Black and Alonzo G. Decker, opened a small machine shop on South Calvert Street in Baltimore City. To do so, Black had to sell his 1907 Maxwell automobile for six hundred dollars, and Decker borrowed the same amount from his grandfather. Their gamble paid off. Only nine years later the company passed the million dollar sales level, and by the end of this decade it may be a billion dollar business.

The key to this success was the development of an electric drill with a pistol grip and trigger switch, two 1914 innovations which are standard on power tools today. In its first years the company had manufactured the products of others, among them a milk bottle cap machine, a postage stamp slitting and coiling machine, a cotton picker, and a candy-dipping machine. In 1916 the company began to manufacture products that the founders had designed themselves: the half-inch portable electric drill and the Lectroflater, a small electric air compressor. Towson became the home of Black & Decker the next year.

The half-inch drill of 1916 was the first of a long and varied line of industrial power tools, and the company grew rapidly. It was the Second World War, however, which sparked the company's movement to tools for the do-it-yourself market. In 1941 Black & Decker began to manufacture fuses, gun shells, and other ordnance for the Allies. Two years later the company received the Army-Navy "E" award for its war efforts, one of four citations it

earned. At the same time the directors were looking ahead to the war's close. To offset an anticipated sharp decline in production, the company decided to produce a line of less powerful, less expensive power tools suitable for the hobbyist and handyman. In fact, there was no decline in business but a boom, a boom which has continued to the present day.

In 1946 Black & Decker introduced the world's first line of popularly priced drills and accessories. It was so successful that by 1951 Black & Decker had produced over one million quarter-inch Home-Utility drills.

Over the years Black & Decker has added to the Home-Utility line. In 1952 the company introduced the finishing sander and the jig saw. In 1957 it expanded the versatility of the Home-Utility line by bringing out the first Black & Decker garden tools—lawn edgers and hedge trimmers.

In 1961 there was still another breakthrough. Black & Decker introduced the world's first cordless electric drill, powered by self-contained nickel-cadmium cells. Black & Decker now foresees the cordless power pack as the basis for many future innovations. The consumer who purchases a single power pack will be able to use it with an ever-enlarging series of attachments, like a vacuum or a lantern—as many as fifty attachments in the years to come.

Black & Decker's first Towson building was a sixty by two hundred-foot frame factory. Over the years other buildings arose as the company grew.

In 1965 the firm ceased to manufacture power tools at the Towson site. Over five

hundred pieces of equipment were transferred to the Hampstead plant—without any loss in production time. Towson remains the administrative headquarters of the company.

Photograph courtesy of Black & Decker

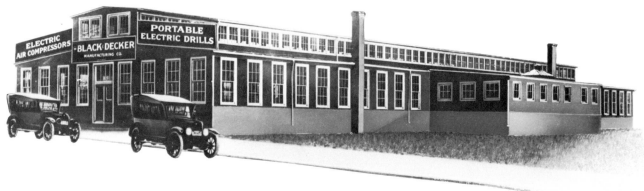

Black & Decker's first half-inch electric drill.
Photograph courtesy of Black & Decker

The Lectroflater filled the demands of a society falling in love with the automobile. It could inflate a thirty-four by four inch tire from dead flat to seventy pounds of pressure in four minutes. But as the air pump became a familiar fixture at gasoline stations, the demand for the Lectroflater dwindled.

Photograph courtesy of Black & Decker

If they didn't make the riveters, these early Rosies may have made the drills during the World War I effort.

Photograph courtesy of Black & Decker

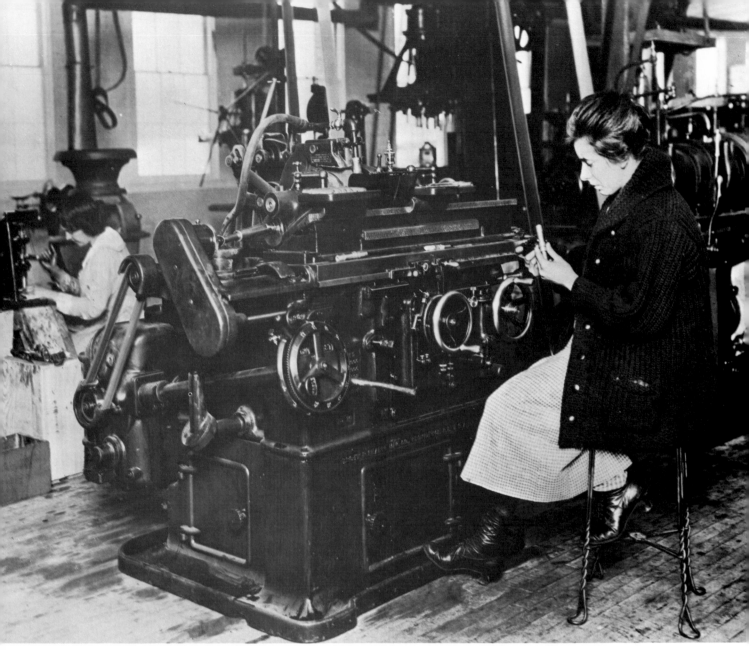

Women workers at the original Towson factory in 1918. The pot-bellied stove which heated the plant is visible in the background.

Photograph courtesy of Black & Decker

The Black & Decker plant was built at Towson Heights on land that had been a farm owned by D. G. McIntosh.

Several factors influenced the founders' decision to move to Towson. First, they believed that a rural environment produced conscientious workers. Second, the Maryland & Pennsylvania Railroad passed the site. In this picture, taken shortly before the Second World War, the Ma & Pa tracks, a siding serving Black & Decker, and the Towson Heights station are visible behind the plant.

Photograph courtesy of Black & Decker

From the company's founding to 1975 four members of the Black and Decker families served as the firm's chief executive officer. Under their leadership, innovation and expansion became Black & Decker characteristics. For example, the company saw the advantages of international production long before overseas expansion became fashionable. A Canadian subsidiary was incorporated in 1922. Today, Black & Decker has seventeen plants outside the United States, and in 1975 overseas business exceeded domestic sales for the first time in the company's history.

Other examples of Black & Decker resourcefulness arose as result of the growth of the company's business in the United States during the 1920s. In 1925 Black & Decker used two Pierce Arrow buses—its "Schoolrooms on Wheels"—to give merchandise demonstrations to distributor salesmen and plant-operating personnel around the country. In 1929 the firm outfitted a Travel-Air monoplane as a flying showroom for products useful in reconditioning aircraft engines. As early as 1921 Black & Decker employed full-page ads in the *Saturday Evening Post*, and in 1955 the company was the first power tool manufacturer to turn to network television advertising to promote sales.

Photographs courtesy of Black & Decker

The founders: S. Duncan Black (1883-1951) and   Alonzo G. Decker (1884-1956).

Robert D. Black   Alonzo G. Decker, Jr.

Perhaps the best symbol of the diversity and invention of Black & Decker is the company's involvement in the United States space program. In 1964 Black & Decker developed a cordless Minimum Torque Reaction Space Tool to be used under weightless flight conditions by astronauts on Project Gemini. Four years later the firm built a flight model of an Apollo Lunar Surface Drill, a battery-operated tool designed to remove core samples from the moon. This drill went to the moon with the Apollo 15 mission in 1971. It operated successfully and was later used on the Apollo 16 and Apollo 17 missions.

Photograph courtesy of Black & Decker

On Cowpens Avenue near Joppa Road, Bruce S. Campbell, son of the company's founder, jockeys a 1912 Mack dump truck. It was the first purchased by the firm, and as Campbell once commented, it took "tough boys in those days," for the truck had no cab, no windshield, and solid tires. Still, it was an improvement on the one hundred mules kept in the Campbell livery stables on East Pennsylvania Avenue.

Campbell joined his father's business in 1908, the year the company was mining stone from the Ridgely quarry for an addition to the Court House. One of the first jobs was to operate a derrick which loaded ton-weight pieces of stone onto a wagon. Once delivered to the Court House, they were hand-cut in the yard.

Photograph courtesy of
Harry T. Campbell Sons' Corporation

Between 1910 and 1917 the Harry T. Campbell Company paved many Towson streets. As early as 1901 Campbell's had begun to produce stone for county road work and by 1903 had contracts to lay roads in some new residential neighborhoods. Not long after moving its headquarters to Towson in 1923, the company became a major supplier of stone and blacktop for county roads.

In the next two decades the firm diversified its product line. In 1934 it purchased its first cement mixer and went into the ready-mixed concrete business. Today Campbell's large mixer trucks are familiar sights on Towson streets. In 1941 the firm began to manufacture Camel-WITE, an important whiting product used in the paint, paper, rubber, and plastic industries. It is most commonly experienced as the fine powder that coats a stick of chewing gum. Finally, in 1945 Campbell's, like Black & Decker, turned to the do-it-yourself trade. The company became the exclusive manufacturers of SAKRETE, a dry, pre-mixed concrete.

A Campbell block. The company supplied the stone for the towered Calvary Baptist Church (far left), concrete and aggregate for the Alexander Brown building (under construction), and, of course, materials for its own headquarters on the corner of Washington and Pennsylvania Avenues. Until that building was completed in 1851, Campbell's main office was in the "little red brick building" on the opposite corner.

Photograph by David E. Turner

Shortly after the building was completed, two generations of the family posed on the front steps. From left to right are H. Guy Campbell, Harry G. Campbell, Jr., Bruce S. Campbell, Jr., S. James Campbell, Richard L. Campbell, and Bruce S. Campbell.

Photograph courtesy of
Harry T. Campbell Sons' Corporation

Harry Tyler Campbell (1859-1922), the founder. A friend's suggestion that there might be more money in the rock on Campbell's farmland than in the cabbages planted there led him to open an old quarry on his property in 1892. When he contracted to supply stone ballast for a new electric streetcar line, his firm was born.

Photograph courtesy of
Harry T. Campbell Sons' Corporation

Supplying mixed concrete for the Alexander Brown building in 1967.

Photograph by David E. Turner

VII. Still A Sleepy Town

Looking northeast from the Maryland State Normal School in the early 1920s. Note the trolley waiting station which sheltered generations of passengers for the Number 8 car. It was replaced by a glass booth in the early 1970s.

Photograph courtesy of Towson State University

York Road looking north past the Maryland State Normal School in 1922. Note the trolley tracks to the right.

Photograph courtesy of LeRoy Y. Haile, Jr.

This graceful stone house is said to date to 1787
and was once the home of Solomon Schmuck,
brother-in-law of William Towson. Shown here
in the late teens, it is today the Valley Gun
Shop. Its lawn is now a blacktop for Gino's
Restaurant at York Road and Investment Place.

Photograph by Charles W. E. Treadwell
Courtesy of Hilda N. Wilson

There had been a Stieber's store on the west side of York Road just below Allegheny Avenue for more than fifty years when this photograph was taken, probably between 1915 and 1917. George H. Stieber constructed this combination residence and store for his shoe manufacturing business in the late 1870s. Later his son began a grocery store there, a family business which has continued to the present day. The younger Stieber is the man in the white coat and butcher's cuffs on the left.

Notable in the foreground of this photograph are the cut limestone curbing and the brick sidewalk in front of Stieber's store, for curbing and sidewalks were still comparatively new arrivals in Towson. The white building reflected in the left window is the Bosley Hotel.

Joseph S. Parker, who worked at Stieber's, stands at the right. Parker went on to establish his own business around the corner on Allegheny Avenue.

Photograph courtesy of Robert T. Parker

Photograph by Carl Behm III

For many residents the firehouse at the intersection of York Road and Dulaney Valley Road was Towson's most prominent landmark. To an earlier generation it was also a monument to the "energy and persistence" of a remarkable Towson businesswoman, Mrs. Mary A. Shealey, who died in 1887 at the age of seventy-four.

The granddaughter of Solomon Schmuck, Mrs. Shealey came to Towson with her uncle, George Shealey. Later she went into business, opening a general store in what had been an old tavern house. From an initial stock of fifteen dollars, she built her establishment into a Towson institution. As her business grew, she moved to a new store near the Odd Fellows' Hall. Her good fortune did not last, however. In 1876 and again in 1878 her business was destroyed by fire. Refusing to give up, she built a "fine and commodious store" at Flat Iron Square on the site of the old tavern in which she had first done business.

Her brick building served the community in a variety of ways. For a time it was an armory for the Towson Guards. And the Towsontown Temperance Society met in its hall, though ironically part of the building later served as a saloon. Here Catholics celebrated the first mass in Towson in 1883. The hall was also used for dances, and Burgoyne's Band practiced in it.

In 1893, twelve years after the first chemical fire companies had been organized in Baltimore County, the building became Towson's firehouse. It replaced an earlier station on East Pennsylvania Avenue. The next year the town acquired water mains and fire plugs, and a Towson Volunteer Fire Department was formed. The bell which hung in the tower called volunteer firemen like the men in this 1920s photograph.

Photograph courtesy of LeRoy Y. Haile, Jr.

Lewis Held's store was an early Towson business. As early as 1874 Held was advertising "Shrewsbury Ice Cream, guaranteed to be ALL CREAM, for the Summer months."

In the 1920s, Maryland State Normal students still snacked at Held's "Goody Shop" at the southwest corner of York Road and Allegheny Avenue. Today Towson State University students frequent its descendant, Souris' Saloon, a favorite watering place.

Photograph courtesy of LeRoy Y. Haile, Jr.

In 1921 pony carts were still on Towson streets, as this picture before the Trinity Church Rectory shows. From left to right, Irwin Galbreath, Frances S. Green, J. Royston Green, Jr., and a friend wait on a Sunday morning.

Photograph courtesy of Frances Steuart Green

In 1888 William A. Lee, the son of John Wesley Lee, invited Towson to "Come see our new store." His advertisements announced the completion of this impressive brick building on the corner of Pennsylvania Avenue and the York Road, which replaced the store destroyed by fire a short time before.

The history of the Lee family on this corner dates to 1863 when John Wesley Lee, who had run an omnibus service between Govanstown and Baltimore City, moved to Towson to manage the depot of the new horse-drawn streetcar line. His interests soon included a general store as well, which operated out of the Odd Fellows' building for a time and then moved to the corner.

Five years after Lee's Store moved into its new building, the streetcar line was electrified and the Court House loop completed. For many years, however, the clock tower on Lee's Store served as a reminder of the horse-car depot that had been there and of the bell which had been rung when a streetcar was about to leave for the city.

Lee's served Towson until 1932. When the photograph on which this drawing is based was taken shortly before the store closed, a loading platform which spanned the length of the Pennsylvania Avenue side of the building had been removed. Once it had been piled high with grains and farm tools. The building itself still stands, although the clock tower is no longer there. It now houses a Hallmark Cards store.

Drawing by Susan Behm

Weekday 1922. York Road was little changed from the turnpike of thirty years before. The road itself had been paved just a few years earlier to accommodate motor traffic, and the Wayside Cross had just been erected to honor those who fell in the Great War.

On the left behind the Wayside Cross stands the Towson Hotel and beside it the Baltimore County Bank. Across York Road is Marley's drug store (with the balcony), the People's Modern Pharmacy on the first floor of the Odd Fellows' Hall, a barber shop, and, on the corner, Lee's Store, with its clock tower barely visible through the trees.

Photograph courtesy of LeRoy Y. Haile, Jr.

Sunday 1975. More notable than the changes in proprietorship or architecture that occurred during the fifty-three years which separate these pictures is a change in mood. Ubiquitous signs remind us that ours is an age of overstatement. As traffic now rushes through Towson, signs leap out to call attention to their businesses. Once businesses spoke for themselves.

Photograph by Carl Behm III

One for a Man, Two for a Horse

Before Towson drug stores became popular in the early 1900s, the town had a long history of practical medicine. Early medical practitioners included tavernkeepers, mothers, traveling medicine men, and veterinarians. Taverns stocked various "headache essences" and L. Vogle sold freckle lotion. But the most persistent medical factotum was the turnpike quack. As early as 1775 one roamed the York Road hawking "Golden Medical Celaphic Snuff," billed to cure everything from dim vision to paralysis to hysteria. "Dr." Horace J. Red also was a popular peripatetic Hippocrates of the early 1800s with his snake root and chestnut bark tea designed to absorb "poisons" in the system. More unpleasant was Red's snake-bite cure. After a scare campaign based on the notion that the woods were infested with venomous snakes, he prescribed cutting up a reptile and applying its skin to the open wound. Always ready to ride, such quacks usually kept their medical offices in an open satchel on a table near a tavern door.

Even after modern pharmacies made their appearance, dangers were rife. People could buy laudanum, for example, without a prescription at Weis' store well after the turn of the century. And during the 1918 flu epidemic, the most popular Towsonian medicine was Dewitt's Cold Tablets with Sherwood's Rye.

For a few days early in the 1900s Towson drug stores did an especially booming business. The run on the pharmacies was occasioned when one Towson resident poured kerosene down an abandoned well to rid it of mosquitoes. The kerosene quickly spread through the maze of underground streams beneath the town. Soon every well tasted of kerosene and upset stomachs were as common as hot tempers.

Advances in medicine and sanitation usually go hand and hand, and so it was in Towson. For example, one of the dozen springs in Towson fed a stream which meandered to the York Road and then under the Ma & Pa bridge. (This stream and the other springs may be seen on the map of 1853.) In fact, this stream was an open sewer which was not covered until 1913. A comprehensive system of sewers and storm drains, planned in 1916, was not completed until 1923.

Advertisement from the 1886 *Baltimore County Union*.

In the Masonic Building at the corner of Washington and Chesapeake Avenues was Asbill's Pharmacy. For many years it was a restful place, cool and quiet, where in the 1960s you could still buy a five cent soda. The building was demolished in 1970 for the Equitable Bank structure.

Drawing by Dolores M. Andrew

The People's Modern Pharmacy of Harry Ryder (right) was on the first floor of the Odd Fellows' Hall.

Photograph by Charles W. E. Treadwell
Courtesy of Hilda N. Wilson

Bullard's Drugless Sanatarium stood on Chesapeake Avenue.

Photograph by Charles W. E. Treadwell
Courtesy of Hilda N. Wilson

York Road in 1917 looking north toward George Pennington's horse-shoeing forge. The large plot inside the fence and the hedge is the current site of Gino's parking lot.

Photograph by Charles W. E. Treadwell
Courtesy of Hilda N. Wilson

"Central!" was the operator's traditional greeting in the days before dials came to Towson. A telephone office was established in 1886, nine years after the *Baltimore County Union* had carried this item: "We had a telephone in Towsontown on Wednesday evening, and a few of our citizens had the pleasure of testing the workings of the new instrument. Conversation was carried on between the Smedley House and the officers of Messrs. Watts and Co., Holliday Street, Baltimore. The telephone is a curious looking little instrument, from its appearance incapable of performing any wonderful things, yet the transmission of sounds through its agency is indeed marvelous."

This stone building on East Pennsylvania Avenue served as Towson's central office from 1906 to 1949. In the same year that Central moved to its present location on the York Road at Linden Terrace, dial phones were first supplied to Towson customers. The Towson dial office was enlarged in 1975.

Photograph courtesy of Towson Library, BCPL

"Every Hour, Every Day." In 1874 Baltimore County formed a police force. By order of the General Assembly, its number was not to exceed thirty constables. Foot patrolmen earned two dollars daily and mounted officers—who provided their own horses—three dollars.

Built in 1926, this police sub-station on Washington Avenue was headquarters for the Baltimore County Police until 1960. In that year headquarters was moved to Bosley Avenue and Kenilworth Drive.

Photograph by Patricia Gehrmann

Greenwood. John E. DeFord completed this neo-Georgian mansion with formal gardens, rolling lawns, and stately trees in 1915. The Greenwood School moved to the estate on Charles Street north of Loyola High School in 1927.

After classes Headmistress Mary A. Elcock watched over her girls' plays, tennis, hockey, and horse events, for Greenwood owned hounds and staged its own hunts and shows. As Deborah B. Morrison recorded, boarders were allowed Saturday visits to Ruxton to spend twenty-five cents; seniors, a more privileged lot, could use their quarters in Towson.

When Miss Elcock retired in 1952, the school closed. Greenwood then became the campus of the Lutheran Deaconess School. In 1966 Greenwood and its acreage became headquarters for the Baltimore County Board of Education.

Photograph by Carl Behm III

The armory, built in 1933.

Photograph by David McElroy

Bowers For Bibliophiles:
The Towson Library

The Towson Library owes its origin to the Woman's Club of Towson. Under the leadership of Louise S. Criblet and Mary Osborn Odell, the library began in the rear of the Odd Fellows' Hall in 1935. Orange crates served as shelves for its collection of one hundred books donated by members of the club.

The library opened to the public in a rented room at 21 West Pennsylvania Avenue on May 1, 1936. By the end of the next year it had moved to a three-room apartment at 420 York Road. For seventeen years, beginning in June 1940, a six-room apartment at 25 West Pennsylvania Avenue was home to the library. In 1957 the library moved to an "interim" location at 28 West Susquehanna Avenue. Another seventeen years passed, however, before the library opened in its present, permanent home on the York Road at East Chesapeake Avenue.

During its earliest years, the library was dependent on the generosity of the Woman's Club, the civic and fraternal organizations in Towson, and interested citizens. Not until 1940 did the County Commissioners assume full responsibility for the library. Eight years later the Towson Library became part of a county-wide library system.

The library has continued to have private support. The Friends of the Towson Library, Inc., formed in 1938 when the project became too large for the Woman's Club to manage alone. Still active today, the Friends invite all those interested in Towson's culture to join. In addition to contributing to the library's holdings, the group currently sponsors lectures, films, and summer programs for children.

Mary Osborn Odell, who was instrumental in creating the first Towson Library, reads to a class of the experimental elementary school at the Maryland State Normal School. Mrs. Odell was the librarian at the college. This photograph was taken in the library of Stephens Hall about 1928.

Mrs. Odell served as librarian when the Woman's Club created the Towson Library. She retained that position until her retirement in 1954.

*Photograph courtesy of
the Woman's Club of Towson*

Organized in 1934, the Woman's Club of Towson set as its goals community service and cultural advancement. Its first project, the establishment of a public library for Towson, was initiated in 1935. During the Second World War the club maintained the largest Red Cross unit in the United States. Its members secured Towson's first STOP signs and planted more than 150 maple and oak trees along Towson's streets. In a recent letter of appreciation to the president of the club, Dr. Robert W. Gibson, the Medical Director of the Sheppard-Pratt

Hospital, cited "the tremendous effort that your group has made through your garden therapy program."

The Woman's Club now meets in what had been the Second Methodist Church. The church was constructed in 1909 for Towson's Methodist Protestant congregation, which had broken away from the Methodist Episcopal church in 1861. Two years after the reunion of the two congregations, the Woman's Club acquired the building in 1954.

Photograph by Maury Feinstein

The austerity and reinforced concrete of contemporary architecture replace the gingerbread and shingles of Victorian construction. This photograph shows the second-level east entrance of the new library. From orange crates and one hundred books, the library has grown into an institution which houses 195,980 volumes and subscribes to 573 periodicals. Its circulation for the fiscal year 1975-1976 exceeded one million volumes.

Photograph by Patricia Gehrmann

1 9 3 6 to 1 9 4 5

TOWSON LIBRARY

and

BALTIMORE COUNTY LIBRARY

ASSOCIATION

25 West Pennsylvania Avenue

Towson, Baltimore Co.

Maryland

This circular describing the hours and services of the Towson Library shows the entrance to the house which the library occupied from 1940 to 1957. A number of Towsonians can recall searching for Plato or Thomas Aquinas in the bathtub, for a lavatory was the philosophy and religion "wing" of the library. The drive-in windows of the Mercantile Safe-Deposit and Trust Company now stand on this site.

Courtesy of John W. McGrain

One Hundred Years of Lumber and Nails

Every Towsonian is familiar with the Stebbins-Anderson Company, a hardware, lumber, and garden supply store. But few realize that the business has operated at the same location for more than a century.

Its history began in 1867, when the Cochrane Lumber Company opened on the west side of the York Road a short distance north of Susquehanna Avenue. The business changed hands—and names—three times before A. D. Stebbins and Edward F. Anderson purchased the entire stock from Harrison Rider in 1911. They incorporated the business as the Stebbins-Anderson Coal and Lumber Company. The name, which has now been shortened, survived a final change of ownership. The Enterprise Fuel Company of Baltimore, founded by J. Walbach Edelen and J. Harry West in 1900,

bought the company in 1926.

When Enterprise acquired Stebbins-Anderson, the business consisted of a lumber yard and a frame sales building. This photograph, taken in 1937, shows the Company's new brick building and the Stebbins-Anderson "fleet," composed of eight trucks.

The longevity of the business can best be appreciated by recalling that when, in 1882, the narrow-gauge railroad built a bridge across York Road just south of the Cochrane Lumber Company, Cochrane had already served Towson for fifteen years. Yet the business has survived the railroad and its bridge, which was dismantled in 1959.

Photograph courtesy of Stebbins-Anderson

The Stamp of Disapproval

A few months after its completion in 1938, the Towson Post Office was mobbed by townsfolk. The attraction there in June 1939 was not stamps, however, though a first-class letter could be mailed for just three cents. Rather, people rushed in to see the new, highly publicized painting that dominated the main partition.

Commissioned by the Works Progress Administration, the mural had been painted by Nicolai Cikovsky, an *emigre* Russian and instructor at Washington's Corcoran Gallery. His theme, suggested by the Baltimore Postmaster, was the development of mail transportation. Accordingly, Cikovsky produced five panels: a covered wagon train leaving a Mississippi River wharf, two square riggers sailing an ocean, a Pony Express rider crossing a desert, a locomotive rounding a bend, and an airplane cutting across the Manhattan skyline.

Almost immediately after its installation, the mural became the object of enraged reviews. *The Jeffersonian* demanded flatly that Towson "get rid of the horrible WPA murals." A *Sun* editorial complained that "No Green Spring Valley horse would claim relationship to the weird steed in the Pony Express scene." Some Towsonians objected that the horse seemed to hop rather than gallop. A seven-year old boy wondered why a capital "I" was dotted. Others mocked the connection of the locomotive's drive rods to its axles, a linking that in reality would knock off the axles rather than propel the engine. The most persistent complaint, however, was that the work gave no sense of the Maryland scene, an insult Old Line State natives found inexcusable.

Cikovsky bemoaned that "you can't satisfy all critics." But mild indifference was the response of the postal clerk who confessed that the mural "doesn't bother us any." Of course his vantage afforded no view of the painting that spans the wall above the service windows.

Photograph by David McElroy

Photograph by Carl Behm III

Keeping Cool

Photograph courtesy of Raymond A. Seitz

In 1940 much of Towson's ice was still being hauled to homes by trucks. Boys followed them eagerly on hot August days to climb aboard, sit on the blocks, and cup handfuls of ice slivers to their mouths while the driver tong-carried blocks into homes without electric refrigeration.

This scene had changed little since the 1870s and 1880s, when young Harry Groom delivered ice and vegetables from his father's farm to Towson residents. Ice was then cut from local ponds or delivered by ship from Maine, one-quarter of the cold load melting away on the voyage south. After opening an ice and ice cream business at York Road and East Chesapeake Avenue, Groom frequently made the five- or six-hour round trip to the Locust Point docks. Only after 1889 did manufactured ice begin to supplement ice harvested in the winter.

In 1909 Clayton Seitz moved to Towson to form the Independent Ice Company, which sold ice manufactured in Baltimore and shipped to Towson every night on a special streetcar. At six o'clock in the morning, Seitz's horse-drawn wagons began their deliveries.

Clayton Seitz stands beside one of his Independent Ice Company wagons soon after opening the Towson business.

Photograph courtesy of Joan Moore

The Seitz ice wagon armadas of 1912 and 1940. In the earlier photograph is the Packard truck purchased for hauling ice from the city. The truck also made home deliveries on the Ruxton route, where the hills could be horse-killers in hot weather. It thus acquired the distinction of being the first motor truck in Maryland used for home ice delivery.

Photographs courtesy of Raymond A. Seitz

No. 7488 **VEHICLE LICENSE** MAR 23 1912
Baltimore, Md.,

1912

CITY OF BALTIMORE, ss.

License is hereby granted to *Independent Ice Co*

No. *Towson Md* Street,

to use and employ for hire within the City of Baltimore, until the first day of January next, his

Number 23900

This License Expires December 31, 1912.

Given under the Corporate Seal of the City of Baltimore in the year nineteen hundred and twelve.

Issued by

for

Collector of Water Rents and Licenses.

TWO HORSE

Courtesy of Raymond A. Seitz

In 1920 Seitz (right) began to manufacture his own ice in a new plant on West Chesapeake Avenue. It could turn out forty-five tons per day by 1942. He renamed his business the Towson Ice Company.

The heart of the ice-making process was the conversion of ammonia from liquid to gas by compression, for this change drew heat from water placed close to the coils of ammonia. The two-and-one-half ton flywheel of the ammonia compressor may be seen behind Seitz. To insure the clarity of the ice, compressors (foreground) circulated cooled air through the tanks of cooling water to remove the air bubbles, which would have given the ice a snowy appearance.

After the water temperature had been reduced to thirteen degrees, the ice was removed from the freezing tanks and stored in a twenty-six degree cold room until delivery.

Photograph courtesy of Raymond A. Seitz

The Penn Hotel was originally built as a private home by Major John Yellott in the early 1870s. After the Yellott family sold it in 1926, it was converted to a hotel-restaurant.

More recently, the Penn Hotel Restaurant—it is no longer a hotel—has been a favorite meeting spot for politicians in Towson, among them Spiro T. Agnew, Dale Anderson, and A. Gordon Boone.

Pictured here, the old house on Pennsylvania Avenue has since been encased within a new addition.

Drawing by Susan Behm

"Now is the Hour." From the late 1930s into the 1950s this house at York Road and Linden Terrace was Virginia Driskill's Fashion Center. During World War II, Mrs. Driskill would provide trousseau, minister, and honeymoon suite for maidens and servicemen eager to marry before a furlough ended. The house was also the scene of many coming-out parties.

When it was built in 1800 by William Bowen, the house was surrounded by over three hundred acres. Since 1935 it has been used commercially. For a time the Colonial Inn and now the Tuxedo House, it will be the entrance to a new shopping mall.

Photograph courtesy of Frederick Furman

On Palm Sunday, 1942, twenty-six inches of wet snow blanketed Towson.

Photograph by Frances Steuart Green

Winning the War: The Myers Company

At 10 West Susquehanna was the Philip Myers Co., an architectural millwork plant founded in 1935. A colonial style frame structure of oiled cypress housed the plant, which in true town fashion employed two and three members of a number of families.

Not an airplane left Glenn L. Martin's during the years of the Second World War without Myers Co. wooden equipment—floor boards for the Martin *Mars,* tail slats for PBMs, turret crates for B26s, and much more. Because Martin aircraft were constructed for the American, British, and Free French, Myers products were frequently in the skies over Europe.

The Myers Co. also manufactured crates for shipment of radar to England during the Battle of Britain. Mr. Myers remembers being led blindfolded for security through Bendix-Friez to write specifications for casing for the new proximity fuse, a major Allied weapon.

Never was a Myers contract late in delivery nor was one of its products rejected during the war years. Employees frequently worked beyond quitting time.

Sold to the John M. Nelson Co. in 1956, the building was later wrecked for the Stebbins-Anderson parking lot.

Glenn L. Martin, the aeronautic magnate, makes the principal address at the awarding of the Army-Navy "E." Mr. Myers, a battle lieutenant during World War I, sits at the right and listens to praise of his plant's contribution to the World War II effort. Mrs. Myers looks on proudly.

Photograph courtesy of Philip Myers

Beneath Allied flags bedecking the Philip Myers Co., Towsonians gather on July 19, 1943. Myers' was the smallest plant—only seventeen employees—to win the coveted Army-Navy "E" for Excellence Award during World War II. And it won the "E" four times. Note the "E" flag flying beneath the national colors and the "V" for victory emblems at the building's front. Such insignia were typical displays of the patriotic war effort from 1941 to 1945.

Photograph courtesy of Philip Myers

York Road looking north in 1922.

Photograph courtesy of Goucher College

single mass migration in history—the rush of
city dwellers to the American suburbs. An
industrial system had been honed during World
War II and now was ready to supply more
products and more jobs for an expanding
nation. Reserves of building provisions,
automotive materials, and fuel, guarded
carefully during the war, were released for
civilian consumption. And land became
immediately available as realtors led buyers
and bulldozers into the country.

York Road in 1962.

Photograph courtesy of Baltimore County

In 1950 the Ma & Pa still chugged across the
State Teachers' College campus, farmland
bordered its south side, and York Road north of
Towson was undeveloped. Anticipating the
growth to suburbia, however, Hutzler's had
begun clearing an area for its store.

Towson's population that year was forty-one
thousand, already nearly double that of ten
years before. By 1960, it was eighty-six
thousand, and by 1970, 102 thousand.

Photograph courtesy of Hutzler's

Here Comes the Number 8!

For all but the most recent generation of Towsonians, a trip downtown meant a ride on the Number 8 streetcar.

Horses pulled the first trolley over the rails between Towson and Baltimore on August 20, 1863, five years after the incorporation of the Baltimore and Yorktown Turnpike Railway Company. One hundred years later streetcars in front of the Towson Court House wait to take passengers down the York Road, perhaps to City Hall in Baltimore or to the shopping district at Fayette and Howard Streets.

Photographs by Herbert H. Harwood

The first streetcars on the Towson line were double-deckers, which served intermittently until 1884. Mary Stieber, who would have been eight or nine when the first streetcar arrived, recalled in 1939: "That was a great day in Towson. Why, one would think that the village was celebrating a national holiday. Everybody went out to see the car come in and the line did a big business for a time—until the novelty wore off." A less happy note, though one equally revealing of the times, is that one of these double-deckers may have been a "Jim Crow" car, with the upper deck enclosed and reserved for black passengers.

Photograph courtesy of the Baltimore Streetcar Museum Library

YORK 4 ROAD

The streetcars were pulled by horses for the first thirty years of service. Nonetheless, because their metal wheels rolled easily over the rails, the cars could carry large numbers of passengers. York Road had steep hills, however, and in places it was necessary to add an additional "hill horse." The boy who tended the "hill horse" would also bring water for the regular team in hot weather or sprinkle sand to improve traction if the road were slippery.

It was the Union Passenger Company which brought the electric trolley to Towson. This company, which soon became part of the City & Suburban Railway Company, purchased the streetcar line from the Baltimore and Yorktown Turnpike Company in 1891. It promised Towson "rapid transit"—the company's phrase—and delivered. In two years Nelson Perin's Company had regraded York Road to eliminate the steepest hills, laid double tracks and the loop at the Court House, and installed overhead electric lines. On April 27, 1893, an electric streetcar left City Hall in Baltimore at noon; thirty-two minutes later, its passengers disembarked in front of the Court House in Towson.

The "convertible" streetcar pictured was among the early electric trolleys on the York Road line. The convertible, so-called because the side windows could be removed and stored during the summer, left passengers defenseless against changes in the weather. The riders cursed their presence on a hot day in January and cursed their absence on a chilly evening in June or during a thunderstorm in August.

*Photograph courtesy of the
Baltimore Streetcar Museum Library*

When this photograph of a "modern" Brill snow sweeper was taken on Chesapeake Avenue in 1958, the car had been in service for more than half a century.

Photograph by John W. McGrain

From its inception the York Road trolley line carried mail to Towson, and in 1868 the Baltimore and Yorktown Turnpike Railway received a contract which called for the delivery of mail between Baltimore and Towson twice each day.

Following Postmaster Warfield's proposal in 1895 that the street railways be used extensively for carrying the mail, special white, blue, and gold postal cars made their debut. These cars ran to Towson during the first decades of this century.

Photograph courtesy of Robert Cardwell

The disadvantages of the convertibles were corrected by the Brill "semi-convertibles," the longest lived of the streetcars which came to Towson. The windows of these cars slid upwards into pockets in the roof and could be raised or lowered as the weather necessitated.

The semi-convertibles were handsome streetcars, red and cream on the outside with brightly varnished wood interiors. The first cars of the type were delivered in 1905.

When this photograph was taken at the Court House loop in 1943, Car 5788 was twenty-five years old. The semi-convertibles had been slated for retirement prior to the Second World War, but an influx of wartime passengers required the company to keep them in service for the duration.

Photograph by Charles T. Mahan

In an effort to lure lost customers away from the automobile and back to the streetcar, a new style of car was designed in 1935. Called the Presidents' Conference Car, after the national meeting of street railway executives which led to its creation, the PCC offered passengers a comfortable seat and a smooth ride.

This PCC is northbound on the York Road just south of Stevenson Lane in October 1963.

Photograph by Herbert H. Harwood

One hundred years after the first horse-drawn trolley made the trip from Baltimore to Towson, buses replaced streetcars on the Number 8 line. The changeover brought to an end the era of streetcars in Baltimore.

Now the whirr of the electric motor, the sparks overhead, safety zones by the tracks, and flattened pennies are only memories, like the horse bells and the bundles of hay that warmed the passengers' feet in a still earlier generation of streetcars.

In this photograph, taken on November 2, 1963, passengers board the streetcar at the Court House loop for a final ride. The last streetcar left Towson at dawn the next morning.

Photograph by John W. McGrain

Looking west in 1950 from the land to be developed
for Hutzler's new store.

Photograph courtesy of Hutzler's

A Modern General Store

Ground-breaking at Hutzler's. Piloting the bulldozer is Albert D. Hutzler (1888-1965). His grandson, Albert III, peeps from behind the man with the scroll. Fire Chief F. Lee Cockey looks on from the rear.

Photograph courtesy of Hutzler's

The Hutzler family has operated its department store in Baltimore since 1858. Following World War II, Hutzler's paced the mass migration to the suburbs. The Towson store was the first of the family's suburban stores. It is pictured here one month after its opening on November 24, 1952.

A second story was added to the parking area in 1963, and the store was enlarged by fifty percent three years later. In 1964, the Rehabilitation and Redevelopment Commission estimated that Hutzler's in Towson had attracted 275 thousand permanent customers.

Photograph courtesy of Hutzler's

Photograph by Michael McIntyre

Goucher College

If conditions for women's education were not bright in Victorian America at large, in the American South they were dark. Many observers thought female education to be destructive of a woman's "sphere." Some believed it to be un-Christian. Many thought college to demand more physical stamina than a woman could give. Still others flatly denied a woman's intellectual equality with a man. And one scholar believed college would make somnambulists of women. For these reasons and more, there were few college preparatory schools for women in the South and none in Maryland.

But there was a glimmer. As in an earlier dark age, it came from the church. The Baltimore Conference of the Methodist Episcopal Church had founded Cokesbury College for boys in Abingdon, Maryland. In a spirit of equality, the Conference planned a similar college for women. Consequently, it founded the Woman's College of Baltimore City in 1885. Later, the first dean described its educational aim as "the formation of womanly character for womanly ends." Gifts of money—much raised by door-to-door campaigns—and land followed, and the college began to rise next to the First Methodist Episcopal Church on St. Paul Street at Lovely Lane. Students were first admitted in 1888 and first graduated in 1892.

Essentially the curriculum was patterned on The Johns Hopkins University's "group system," in which students were free to choose one of four courses: classical, modern languages, natural sciences, or mathematics. Those who had insufficient earlier training were expected to complete college preparatory courses before acceptance into the regular curriculum.

From the beginning a college spirit prevailed, as if generated spontaneously. Students wrote college yells and school songs, developed class rivalries, and chose class colors and flowers. Between the students and faculty a comradeship developed, the professors often hosting teas and Christmas parties for the young scholars and always being available for consultation.

The Etruscan Revival halls of the first campus were built on a cornfield. This picture from around 1915 shows the St. Paul Street side. By 1920 Goucher owned or controlled twenty-six buildings.

Photograph courtesy of Goucher College

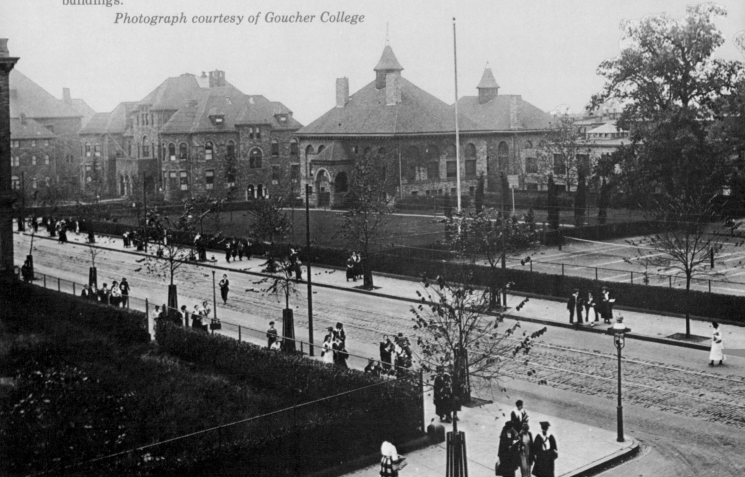

A recent picture of the Dulaney Valley Road and Fairmount Avenue junction. Commercial development encroaches on residential north Towson. In the lower left sector is the Dulaney Valley Shopping Center. Above it are the Dulaney Valley Apartments. At the lower right is the parking lot of the Towson Plaza Shopping Center. North of it is Goucher College, hidden in the foliage. The Towson Methodist Church, consecrated in 1957, rests before the Loch Raven lakes.

Photograph courtesy of Hilda N. Wilson

Claiming the new campus at Dulaney Valley Road in 1921.

Photographs courtesy of Goucher College

A four-year liberal arts curriculum has always been central at Goucher. In the early years, students who wished to specialize in art, music, or elocution were required to spend more time for their degrees. Here, a French class meets in 1903 or 1904. The artists are from the same time.

Photographs courtesy of Goucher College

Picnics were always pleasant interludes for the early Goucher students. The outings at President Goucher's home on Reisterstown Road, Alto Dale, developed into the May Day event held annually from 1920 to 1935. It featured pageants, dancing, the daisy chain, and the crowning of the May Queen.

These scenes, from the early 1900s and 1935, are at Alto Dale and Towson respectively.

Photographs courtesy of Goucher College

With a social calendar as busy as their academic one, these 1942 students gather in a date parlor in Mary Fisher Hall, first building on the Towson campus.

Photograph courtesy of Goucher College

A moonlight serenade.

Photograph courtesy of Goucher College

A dance in the 1950s.

The bonfire is traditional at Goucher. The purpose of this one in the 1940s is uncertain, but from 1915 to 1932 seniors built a "funeral pyre." On it they sacrificed the "hates" of their college days; everything from text books to alarm clocks was tossed into the flames.

A Rich Curriculum

Besides courses in the traditional lecture hall and seminar, Goucher students gain practical experience in their academic majors.

Photographs courtesy of Goucher College

Dancing for a degree. Established as a major in 1975, the dance curriculum at Goucher can be combined with a theater option.

Photograph courtesy of Goucher College

Goucher's course in historic preservation, started in 1975, is one of just two such under-graduate programs in the United States. In this picture Professor Julie Roy Jeffrey, left, discusses the restoration of the stucco facade with class members at Hampton House.

Photograph courtesy of Goucher College

On the campus.

Photograph courtesy of Goucher College

Riding has long been a favorite course of
Goucher students. Some stable their own horses
on the campus.

Photograph courtesy of Goucher College

The first woman president of Goucher College,
Rhoda M. Dorsey, took office in 1974. A
demanding, innovative, and popular professor
of history, two of Dr. Dorsey's more celebrated
courses were "Cowboys and Indians" and
"Historical Geography," which included blindfolded tests on topographical maps.

*Photograph by Robert de Gast
Courtesy of Goucher College*

Private school, public benefit. Two women walk toward Kraushaar Auditorium. Completed in 1962, the one thousand-seat building serves equally as lecture hall and civic center. Here the Baltimore Symphony Orchestra performs regularly, and touring orchestras, chamber ensembles, and dance troupes complement its active concert season.

Unearthed in 1951, the cannon once stood on the grounds of Epsom, the estate which the college bought from the Chew family. It is now mounted in front of the Julia Rodgers Library.

President of Goucher from 1948 to 1967, Otto F. Kraushaar, right, walks in an academic procession with President Milton S. Eisenhower of The Johns Hopkins University. A pre-eminent blend of teacher-scholar-administrator, Dr. Kraushaar led Goucher through its first years on the Towson campus.

The Towson campus today is what was envisioned in 1921—an academic preserve hedged with trees and shrubbery. Deer traverse the grounds, and red foxes, raccoons, possum, groundhogs, and rabbits abound. Quiet and comfortable, it is a civil place where nine hundred students and eighty professors learn together.

*Photograph by M. E. Warren
Courtesy of Goucher College*

Photograph courtesy of Goucher College

189

Main Street in the 1950s.
*Photograph courtesy of Baltimore County
Board of Education*

The Dance of the Cranes

During the fifteen years between 1945 and 1960, the heart of tiny Towson pounded to keep pace with new demands on its resources. Because its street plan was virtually the same in the 1950s as it had been in 1862, traffic jams were customary. Motorists cursed the slow movement around the firehouse, which clotted one of the busiest intersections in Baltimore County, the junction of York, Joppa, and Dulaney Valley Roads. Housing in East Towson was a scar; many units there still lacked indoor plumbing. Community services became debilitated; the library, schools, fire and police stations, and transit facilities strained under the new stresses on them. Lack of a central plan permitted general congestion, poor landscaping, and architectural misfits.

Government recognized Towson's problems. In 1961 the General Assembly authorized the County to carry out urban renewal activities. By 1964 the federal government had allocated nine million dollars for various phases of planned community development. Baltimore County appointed the Rehabilitation and Redevelopment Commission. It hired consultants and surveyed land use, architecture, families, utilities, and population.

The Commission saw Towson as ideal for redevelopment: a small core bounded by strong "planning anchors"—Goucher College, Towson State University, three hospitals, Black & Decker, and many stable residential areas. Redevelopment would renew this small urban core, making it consistent with the strength of its surrounding areas. Governmental money was waiting. Only approval by the voters was needed for a demolition bond of four million dollars sought by the Spiro Agnew administration. With it urban renewal could begin.

But opposition loomed. Three groups—the "Committee to Save Our Homes," "Baltimore County Citizens," and "Maryland Petition Committee"—attacked the Rehabilitation and Redevelopment Commission's arbitrary condemnation rights, stressed the pressures on small businesses to relocate, and warned of higher taxes. East Towson's black community also objected. These forces won the day; they defeated the bond issue and thus the urban renewal plan. Traffic congestion, substandard buildings, poorly laid-out lots, inadequate parking, and mixed land use continued. Possible tax revenues from revitalized businesses were lost. More importantly, Towson's random development continued as more cranes moved in.

Photograph by David E. Turner

"Nor shall my sword": The Redevelopment and Rehabilitation Commission's vision of "a new Towson." Confronted with the existence of outdoor privies in east Towson in the 1960s and 241 substandard structures, the Commission campaigned for citizen acceptance of this preliminary plan in 1964. It features a tunnel from York Road to Chesapeake Avenue to Dulaney Valley Road and a ring road to carry through traffic around the center of Towson. The planners also proposed new shops, a department store, and banks; a new recreation center, library and theater; new residences; and parks and an open plaza. The commission argued that the locally controlled program would not only improve the quality of life in Towson but would also provide economic reward by raising the assessed value of taxable property in the urban renewal area from about twenty-one million dollars in 1963 to seventy million dollars by 1975.

Photograph courtesy of Baltimore County

Built in 1871, the First Methodist Church on York Road was demolished to make way for the Investment Building in 1964. "Future developments" would prove that "Towson's most spectacular building" was a very modest high-rise indeed.

Photograph by David E. Turner

A final addition to the original Court House was completed in 1958, but at that time there was no evidence of the changes to come ten years later. Instead, Court House Square radiated peace, harmony, and graceful dignity, as in this view from the Court House lawn to the J. B. Longnecker house at the corner of Baltimore and Pennsylvania Avenues.

Photograph by John W. McGrain

Eminent domain, imminent destruction. After the site of the new courts building had been determined, all of the homes along Baltimore Avenue between Pennsylvania and Chesapeake Avenues were vacated by 1968, before the

wrecking ball swung. Space will abound in the new legal emporium, with twelve courtrooms proposed to accommodate the County's ten judges.

Photographs by David E. Turner

A recent view of Towson State University with its Residence Tower. The new courts building and the Bosley Avenue bypass are under construction.

Some portions of the Redevelopment and Rehabilitation Commission's vision have come into being. New bank and office buildings line Washington Avenue at Court House Square and portions of a ring road around Towson have been constructed to alleviate congestion on the York Road. Completed first was Fairmount Avenue, which links the York Road north of Towson with Joppa Road on the east. In 1972 clearing and grading had begun on the western perimeter of the loop. Bosley Avenue, once a residential street lined with tall trees, is being widened to a six-lane thoroughfare to connect the York Road at Burke Avenue with Towsontown Boulevard and Fairmount Avenue north of Towson.

Photograph courtesy of Towson State University

Towsonian Spiro T. Agnew was elected Vice President of the United States in 1968 when he was fifty years old. A lawyer, his rise to the high office was swift. After serving as president of the Loch Raven Kiwanis Club and the Loch Raven School PTA, Agnew was appointed to the Baltimore County Zoning Board. In 1962 he was elected County Executive and in 1966 Governor of Maryland. While County Executive, Agnew was a strong advocate for urban renewal in Towson. While Vice President, he was known for his strong attacks on "effete intellectual snobs" and "nattering nabobs of negativism." A powerful orator, he was a strong advocate in his speeches for law and order. After pleading *nolo contendere* to charges of tax evasion on payments made to him by Maryland building contractors, Agnew was sentenced to three years' probation and was fined ten thousand dollars. Mr. Agnew resigned from the Vice Presidency in 1973.

Photograph from the files of
*the **Towson Times***

Hilda N. Wilson has written that when she first came to Towson in 1922 to attend the State Normal School, the town had "hitching rails and the air of a bazaar." Since then she has become an active partner with her husband in the Wilson Electric Company and a leader of Towson's business community. Through the Towson Business Association she has encouraged Towson's economic growth while seeking to preserve the heritage and beauty of the town's past. Her booklet, "Towson: Then—Now," and the annual Towsontown Spring Festival are but two of her many contributions to the community. Her honors include selection as Towson's Woman of the Year, the naming of the new library's public meeting room in her honor, and designation as an outstanding alumna of Towson State University.

Photograph courtesy of
the Wilson Electric Company, Inc.

Survivor but refugee. Constructed prior to 1869 at Washington and Pennsylvania Avenues, the "little red brick building" was originally the law office of Colonel D. G. McIntosh. Later, it briefly housed the Towson National Bank, and ironically a descendant of the bank made the old building a *cause celebre*. Because the Mercantile Safe-Deposit and Trust Company wanted a new high-rise building, there was talk of its wrecking the little office. But after a popular conservation effort, the building was moved to the grounds of the Towson YMCA.

When this picture was taken in 1968, the "little red brick building" was occupied by the Towson Chamber of Commerce. In the background is Loyola Federal, Towson's first high-rise bank, built in 1959.

Photograph by David E. Turner

As the curious looked on, the wrecking ball swung in 1968. An unusual aspect of the old Mercantile bank's demolition was that the marble-front facade stood until the very end. A fourteen-story office building and bank replaced it.

Photograph by David E. Turner

After ninety years the Mt. Moriah Masonic Hall awaits demolition in 1970 as the steel of the Mercantile building rises behind it.

Photograph by David E. Turner

These two-and-one-half story houses on Allegheny Avenue await demolition in 1973. Since 1960 there has been virtually no individual home construction in central Towson. Instead, high-rise apartments and condominiums have thrust into the Towson skies.

Photograph by David E. Turner

Surgery for Towson—or a bomb?

Photograph by David E. Turner

Vertical Living

The Penthouse, a twenty-eight-story
condominium, was completed in 1976.
Photograph by Patricia Gehrmann

When construction on a nearby high-rise began, this home on East Pennsylvania Avenue was wrecked not long after its picture was taken in 1967.

Photograph by David E. Turner

A frame and shingle house at Chesapeake and Baltimore Avenues in 1975.

Photograph by Patricia Gehrmann

On February 19, 1887, the *Baltimore County Union* announced that "Mr. Lewis H. Urban is having plans prepared for a pretty frame cottage which he proposes to erect on the south side of his lot, fronting the turnpike. Work will commence as soon as Spring opens." An 1853 plat of Towson shows the Urbans already occupying what became the southeast corner of York Road and Pennsylvania Avenue, where they etablished a popular tavern.

The Urban house was sacrificed for a public blacktop.

Photograph by David E. Turner

The stucco-over-stone Lee-Massenberg house at Pennsylvania and Delaware, 1975.

Photograph by Carl Behm III

Photograph by David E. Turner

A New Skyline

A view to the northeast from the Ridgely. On
the left is Hampton Plaza, another new high-
rise dwelling, and the Grempler Realty
Company Building on Joppa Road.

In the twenty-eight story Ridgely, in 1976, a
condominium unit cost from forty-three
thousand dollars to sixty-five thousand dollars.
In 1850 the *Baltimore County Advocate*
advertised some land northeast of Towson: "304
acres on Gunpowder for sale, 90 cleared, $5,000,
half in cash, balance in 6, 12, and 18 mos.
Frame dwelling, outbuildings, orchard, timber,
house on hill."

Photograph by Carl Behm III

To the west, the view is dominated by the Washington Avenue parking garage, the Chesapeake Avenue parking garage with the vertical thrust of the Equitable Bank behind it, and, in the center of the picture, the Mercantile building. To the west of it is the new Courts Building. Loyola Federal bank, Alexander Brown investment building, and the Allegheny Avenue parking garage complete the line.

The parking temples and high-rises are signs of contemporary realty: Land is expensive; the sky is free.

Photograph by Carl Behm III

Postscript

For better and worse, Towson's history had been determined by its roads. The town was born at the crossing of Joppa Road, the Indian trail which became an important east-west route to the eighteenth-century provincial capital at Joppa, and the York Road, the north-south link between the port of Baltimore and the farmlands of Pennsylvania. True to its birth, Towson has let politics and business shape its course ever since. Ezekiel Towson no doubt recognized the profits to be had from the traffic on these roads when he built his tavern at their intersection in 1768. And in 1854 Towson's accessibility contributed to its selection as the seat of government for Baltimore County.

Like an asphalt river that slows at Towson and then wanders north into more spacious lands, the York Road has always generated new businesses. At first, it was responsible for Towson's growth and prosperity. Now it is contributing to Towson's decline. While development in the town continues haphazardly, uncontrolled by any central plan or sense of community, the rural land to the north beckons speculators. Businesses inch farther and farther northward. It seems, in fact, that a new shopping center appears at a York Road intersection every year. The latest proposal describes this syndrome in its name, "The Hunt Valley Shopping Center." What once were green fox-hunting fields may soon be a lake of blacktop surrounding an island of concrete stores. Yet with each new shopping center a bit of old Towson dies. Recently, the pressure of a flood of traffic northward bound on the York Road cut a new channel around the town. The completion of the Towson bypass in 1975 warns that Towson's main street may someday become a stagnant backwater.

If Towson has not reconciled its architectural contradictions, it has grown comfortable with them. Behind this gracious white frame house at Washington and Allegheny Avenues looms the Allegheny Parking Garage, a privately operated facility.

Photograph by Carl Behm III

Acknowledgements

We wish to thank all those who lent us pictures, for without their generosity this book would have been impossible. Their names appear with the pictures they lent, not only as credits for the pictures but also as an acknowledgement of their time and hospitality.

Special mention must be made of the photographs of the late Charles W. E. Treadwell, however. Photographing Towson as early as the teens of this century, he produced a valuable record of Towson life. Fortunately, many of his negatives have been preserved by Hilda N. Wilson, who lent them to us for this book.

Thanks are also due to those who helped us in other ways, through their memories, their encouragement, their wit, their expertise, and always their graciousness: to Herbert D. Andrews, Jean Atkinson, William R. Brown, Whitney Christian, Joseph W. Cox, R. A. Dieffenbach, Glorian D. Dorsey, W. Michael Dunne, Jr., John W. Edelen, Frank E. Farnan, George S. Friedman, Wolfgang Fuchs, Elizabeth Gessford, Robert Greenfield, Mrs. Russell Hall, Albert D. Hutzler III, Dan L. Jones, Charlotte Kakel, Katherine Klier, Charles B. Leach, Jr., Joseph A. McManus, George Nixon, Elmer Parks, Gary W. Parks, Marcus E. Pollock, Sue Richardson, Kingsley Smith, Frank Stricklin, Priscilla Tainter, Bernard G. Taylor, Virginia Thompson, Margaret Turnbull, Nancy West, John L. Wighton, Jack Wulfert, Merle Yoder, and Mrs. Clyde Young; and especially to James Karmrodt Lightner, Christine Veselik, and David McElroy, photographers whose skills in the darkroom made our days brighter.

For her encouragement, patience, and careful reading, we owe a great debt to our editor at The Donning Company, Donna Reiss Friedman.

Finally, our special thanks go to The Friends of the Towson Library, Inc., which provided us with a much-needed measure of financial support.